Hearing and Knowing

Theological Reflections
on Christianity in Africa

Mercy Amba Oduyoye

WIPF *&* STOCK · Eugene, Oregon

Wipf and Stock Publishers
199 W 8th Ave, Suite 3
Eugene, OR 97401

Hearing and Knowing
Theological Reflections on Christianity in Africa
By Oduyoye, Mercy A.
Copyright©1986 Orbis Books
ISBN 13: 978-1-60608-861-6
Publication date 6/8/2009
Previously published by Orbis Books, 1986

"It is no longer because of your words that we believe, for we have heard for ourselves, and we know that this is indeed the Savior of the world."

John 4:42

Contents

iv

Preface

These essays on African Christian theology describe some of the theological understandings to which I have come in my journey over the years from dogmatics to membership in the Ecumenical Association of Third World Theologians (EATWOT) and the Ecumenical Association of African Theologians (EAAT). I have not set out to give an account of systematic theology in Africa. I intend to express something of the belief of the people who belong to these two organizations: that theology is for living. These essays thus are aimed at sharing with you aspects of the Christian faith that I, an African, find compelling—to the extent that I have understood and appropriated that faith. You will not find here a panorama of African expression of Christian theology—only the content of my hope and my reason for holding firmly to the faith delivered to the nations and to the religion of Jesus of Nazareth designated Son of God with power.

I have written from the standpoint that there is no justification for demanding one uniform system of theology throughout the Christian community, but that theology reflects awareness of the horizon toward which all believers move. I hope I shall be able to articulate what I believe to be the essence of the Christian faith: that our lives are hidden in God. The Akan name for the Creeper Commelina Nudifbra, or Benghalensis, flower expresses this in another way. The Commelina folds up its leaves whenever it is touched. It sleeps, or closes its eyes. It "never dies" for God's life constantly renews its life. J. B. Danquah translates the creeper's name as "Could God die, I would die."

"Unsystematic" as these essays are, I count on them to give some idea of the theological issues we in Africa face and some impetus toward further articulation of the faith. While I call these insights and reflections "mine" and take full responsibility for them, I cannot claim that they are new or that they have been revealed to me exclusively. The experiences that have molded my theological orientation have been many and varied. I am sure that those people I have met, heard, or whose writings I have read will find themselves in these essays. I ask the pardon of any who have not been acknowledged appropriately. I wish to express my appreciation specifically to my mother and father, my first theological teachers; to Noel King, who directed me to formal theological studies; and to C. G. Baeta and Maurice Wiles, whose different paths to faith have made me stop and work out my own. I do not hold any of these people responsible for the positions I have taken. I have appropriated their insights into the context of the life of doxology we are all called to live. My gratitude goes to Selly Oak Colleges—to the president, the dean of missions, and the staff—for enabling me to test these thoughts in an ecumenical and international context, and to the University of Ibadan for granting the Sabbatical leave 1981/ 82 spent at Selly Oak.

MERCY AMBA ODUYOYE

Introduction

THE LIBERATION OF THEOLOGY

There was a time when the only acceptable adjective to append to the word *theology* (apart from confessional words like Lutheran or Anglican) was the word *German*. "German" theology was recognized as having a flavor all its own, unlike, for example, "British" or "American." In those days before the turbulent 1960s, Asian theology, black theology, water-buffalo theology, and so on, did not exist as recognizable bodies of distinctive Christian thought. Indeed, they could not have existed, for "Christian" theology was considered an all-inclusive entity. Bearing no direct relationship to its geographical or human source, it was "made in heaven" for the consumption of the whole earth.

Now we are beginning to talk of "Third World theology." What exactly is this "Third World theology"? The combination of the two ideas—"Third World" and "theology"—is an unhappy but an unavoidable one. The term "Third World" is regarded as a heresy by some. There is only One World, they claim. To others, the term is suspect because it connotes third place in a hierarchy of worlds. Still others point out that the geographical restriction inherent in the term makes it untenable. They maintain that there is really a Third World within the First and a First World within the Third. For them the term refers to all those who are exploited by capitalism, imperialism, colonialism, racism (and recently, sexism) as distinct from those who benefit from these "isms." Further, all this has an economic base. The debate on the meaning of "Third World" usually excludes any consideration of the Second World and concentrates on pitting the material affluence of the capitalist

West against the material poverty of the "Third World."

Combined with the word "theology," "Third World" refers to the world of the oppressed, the majority of whom are to be found in the areas defined as the Third World by the Bandung Conference of 1955. The term also refers to Blacks in the Americas, Native Americans, the aborigines of Australia, the Maoris of New Zealand, and the peoples of the oceanic areas of the world, such as the Caribbean and the Pacific Islands.[1] Because of the intricate nature of oppression throughout the world, the concept of the Third World is not limited by geography. All who do theology from the context of injustice and unrighteousness—feminists, for example—find themselves at home among Third World theologians.

What is theology? To answer this question one would have to write a book; several have indeed been written on the subject (see Wiles 1976). Suffice it to say that Christian theology is done wherever people reflect on their life situation in the context of the gospel. Hence the various expressions of Christian theology are sometimes referred to as contextual theology. This Introduction will serve to explain the background, the spring, from which the reflections offered in this book flow.

The 1960s saw the peak of the independence movements by which African countries struggled to extricate themselves from the entanglements of colonial rule. That decade saw other types of liberation movements too. Students in universities and high schools, Blacks in the United States, and women (mostly Euro-Americans) organized and demanded their rights. Authority was in crisis everywhere. Not even the living God escaped debate as philosophers and theologians queried the language we use in talking about God. In this atmosphere dogmatic theology and church discipline came under heavy criticism.

In church circles in Africa the idea of missions and the presence of missionaries came under fire. Missionaries, of different color and foreign nationality, were asked to go with the colonial governors back to their homeland. The Division (later Commission) of World Mission and Evangelism of the World Council of Churches called attention to this change in a statutory conference (Mexico, 1963). The members of that conference redefined the mission of the church, explaining it as a movement both to and from the six continents. Each church in each area of the world, they said, is both a sending and a receiving community. There are no longer "mission fields" and "missionary" churches, but "partners in mission." Christianity has no seat in Europe from which emanate all missionaries and all theological wisdom (see Fey 1976, 193–195).

THIRD WORLD THEOLOGIES

Liberation had come to the missionary movement. It was followed closely by the liberation of Christian theology. Not until the publication of Juan Segundo's book, *The Liberation of Theology* (Buenos Aires, 1975), however, was this stand publicly asserted (see Segundo 1976). Theologians throughout the world who felt a call to speak more relevantly to their age and generation freed themselves from traditional dogmatic and systematic theology and focused on life issues. Instead of telling people what questions to ask and then furnishing them with the answers, theologians began to listen to the questions people were asking and then seek the answers.

In 1973 Gustavo Gutiérrez, a Peruvian, published his book *A Theology of Liberation* (Gutiérrez 1973; Peruvian edition, 1971). The books of Gutiérrez and Segundo and the Conference of Latin American Bishops—particularly that held in Medellín in 1968—brought what was christened "liberation theology" to the attention of theologians and theological schools everywhere.

C. G. Baëta, a Ghanaian theologian, called liberation theology "a peculiarly Latin American product."[2] I maintain, however, that liberation theology is not really peculiar to Latin America. Quite a body of theological works exists that accepts the validity of freeing Christian thought from traditional dogmatic expressions. In Great Britain, J. A. T. Robinson, John Hick, and others are calling Christians to wake up to the expression of their living faith in living terms. Both theo-logy and christology are under review.[3]

In Africa this liberation of theology has borne a variety of fruits. In South Africa a series of conferences on black theology was held in 1971. The collection of lectures given at these conferences was published by the University Christian Movement (1972) in South Africa and then was quickly banned in that country. Another conference held under the auspices of the Missiological Institute at

Lutheran Theological College (Mapumulo, Natal, 1972) took up the theme "Relevant Theology for Africa."[4] The theologians associated with these deliberations and writings were later to become closely linked with the Black Consciousness movement of South Africa for which Steve Biko died (see Biko 1973). Like the Latin American version, this liberation theology was no disengaged, neat, systematic schema of Christian belief; it was not written by academic theologians employing "careful balance" and "cautiously picked vocabulary." It was the faith of a people under pressure calling on Blacks "to throw off their internal enslavement as a necessary preliminary to throwing off external enslavement" (Moore 1973, viii). It was a theology born from a situation in which "the Christian church has been a powerful instrument in making possible the political oppression of black people" (ibid.). Naturally the traditional theological and linguistic symbols of white Christianity were all suspect, and fresh language had to be created to use in telling and living the gospel of Jesus Christ.

The title of the book *Black Theology: The South African Voice* (Moore 1973) suggests the existence of other voices in black theology. Black theology in the United States developed in the atmosphere of the Black Power movement of the 1960s and of the liberation movement led by Martin Luther King. This nascent theology was nursed by, among others, James Cone, whose *God of the Oppressed* summarizes much of what liberation theology is about. Cone pointed out that black theology was as old as the presence of black Christians in the United States.

Another type of African Christian theology was being experienced in Africa. African traditional religion, which had been presented in missionary letters as "gods in retreat," was fast becoming a "battle of the gods." Okot p'Bitek and other Africanist scholars pointed out the superiority of African natural religion to Christianity (p'Bitek 1970).

A consultation on "Biblical Revelation and African Beliefs" was held (Ibadan, 1966) under the auspices of the All Africa Conference of Churches (AACC) (see Dickson and Ellingworth 1968). It followed the Second Assembly (1963) at which several theologians expressed their feeling that

the church in Africa could only attain selfhood and be adequate for [its] mission, when [it] possessed a first-hand knowledge of the Lord of the Church and was able to express that knowledge in clear accents, made possible through [its] own original meditation and thinking [Dickson and Ellingworth 1968, 9].

The AACC consultation had predecessors in the effort toward "original meditation and thinking." Idowu's *Towards an Indigenous Church* had been published in 1965 (London). The faculty of theology in Kinshasha had led discussions in the early 1960s and published articles such as "Débat sur la théologie Africaine" (1961) and "Nouvelle revue de science missionaire" (1962). The Ibadan consultation was, however, rightly described as

> an expression of a deep longing that the churches of Africa might have an opportunity of thinking together of the faith which had come tó them from the older churches of the West and through missionaries of a different cultural background who, in the nature of things, could not fully appreciate the reactions of their converts to their faith in the light of their own traditional beliefs and practices [Dickson and Ellingworth 1968, vii].

All these events and publications were attempts to liberate African Christians from "predigested" theologies so that they might become creative and relevant. Like the Samaritans at the well, African theologians are now saying to their tutors: "It is no longer because of your words that we believe, for we have heard for ourselves, and we know that this is indeed the Savior of the world" (Jn 4:42). Scholars, in teams and individually, searched for existing theological writings of African Christians and contributed their own insights. These efforts, along with the "selfhood movement" of the churches and the impetus of the ecumenical movement were the sources of an African movement toward a relevant theology.

Theological insight from Asia is also a part of Third World theology. Asian theologians have an important voice in the Ecumenical Association of Third World Theologians. Aloysius Pieris, S.J., and Tissa Balasuriya, both from Sri Lanka, would say that there has been Asian Christian theology for as long as there have been Asian Christians. The story of the breakthrough in Asian theology is similar tó the African story, with one important difference. Western Christianity, awed by the antiquity of Asian religions, did not dare to feign superiority over them. The West felt confident that the religion contained in Hebrew Scriptures and the Christian Testament was superior to African religion; but were a bit diffident when confronted with Asian religions.

This historical hesitancy where Asian religions are concerned has resulted in some striking differences between the African and the Asian versions of a liberating theology. Nevertheless, the common search for relevance, especially as related to indigenous spirituality, stimulates joint projects.

ECUMENICAL ASSOCIATION OF THIRD WORLD THEOLOGIANS (EATWOT)

Third World theologians brought their varied backgrounds to a common association. The Ecumenical Association of Third World Theologians (EATWOT) was born in Africa after a consultation ("An Ecumenical Dialogue of Third World Theologians," Dar es Salaam, Aug. 5–12, 1976) attended by theologians from Africa, Asia, Latin America, and the United States. The participants represented confessional families, including Roman Catholic and Orthodox churches. The theme for the dialogue was "The Significance of Theology in the Countries of the Third World."

Two streams of theological exploration came together at that consultation. One issued from the University of Louvain, where between January 1975 and August 1976 a provisional preparatory committee made up of students from the three continents began the search for like-minded colleagues in Africa. The second came from Latin American theologians who wanted to meet with other Third World theologians. This desire was first expressed at the Theology of the Americas conference (Detroit, 1975). Those who attended the meeting held at Louvain in 1975 resolved to benefit from the occasion of the Fifth Assembly of the World Council of Churches (Nairobi, 1976) and make further contacts. They chose a steering committee made up of representatives from India (J. Russell Chandran), Zaïre (Ngindu Mushete), South Africa (Manas Buthelezi), Mexico (Enrique Dussel), Argentina (José Míguez Bonino), India (D. S. Amalorpavadass), and Chile (Sergio Torres) (see Fabella and Torres 1977, xii–xxiii; 1–6).

Theirs was not an easy meeting. The convergence of interests and thinking was apparent, but differences were also real and several times threatened to cause division. One elder Christian statesman of Africa, Julius Nyerere, saw the potential of such an association. He enthusiastically lent his support and encouragement to its development, for he knew that Christians of the Third World should have a chance to explain how they understand the meaning of revelation in the midst of poverty and underdevelopment.

A declaration was issued calling on all who were doing theological work to reflect on the concerns and findings of the consultation and to join in the building up of a more righteous world. The hope was that all those who believe in Christ might be drawn into the struggle for the realization of a New World Order and a New Humanity (Fabella and Torres 1977, 259). Whatever name they call themselves or may be called by others, those who have joined the Ecumenical Association of Third World Theologians can all be considered "liberation theologians." I will use that designation in this generic way throughout these essays.

EATWOT's first assembly was held in Accra (1977), the fifth in New Delhi (August 1981). Consultations, research seminars, and practical involvement brought these women and men together. Their struggle for justice involved not only academic theologians but other church people as well. Study sessions at the New Delhi meeting were held under the title "Irruption of the Third World: Challenge to Theology."[5]

THE ECUMENICAL ASSOCIATION OF AFRICAN THEOLOGIANS

The Africans present at the Accra meeting of EATWOT (1977) concluded that some formal organ was needed in order to encourage the involvement of more Africans in the movement for a relevant theology. Theological associations did already exist in Africa, but to serve the specific ethos of a liberating theology that could affect the life of the church and respond to societal issues these theologians realized that something new was needed. This realization led to the calling of a consultation of African theologians at Yaounde (September 1980). There the Ecumenical Association of African Theologians (EAAT) was formally inaugurated.

The deliberations of this meeting as well as articles written by African theologians are published by the Association's *Bulletin of African Theology* (Kinshasha).

Several persons and organizations, though not members of the associations described above, are closely related to them in thinking and give them moral support: Dom Helder Camara, a Brazilian Roman Catholic bishop; M. M. Thomas of India, president of the World Council of Churches; Burgess Carr, former general secretary of the All Africa Conference of Churches (AACC); and the AACC itself.

Dialogue has begun between these theological associations in the Third World and theologians in Europe who wish to reexamine their own context. In December 1981 the first formal dialogue between them took place in the Netherlands under the theme "The Future of Europe, a Challenge to Theology." Other European theologians have expressed a specific interest in conversations with the Africa Association of Theologians.

THE AFRICAN THEOLOGIAN TODAY

My experiences with these groups of theologians have influenced the shape of these essays, but they are not summaries of one conference or another. The essays come out of my African experience, but they are not summaries of what Africans are saying. They are my own contribution toward expanding our common horizon.

Anyone doing theology in Africa has to take all of Africa's background into account. Both the method and the content of one's work are influenced by it. This is not to say that the pull of denominationalism and the heavy reliance on Western theological categories and expressions have suddenly disappeared from Africa. The "selfhood of the church" much talked of in the 1960s has been slow to materialize, and the call for a moratorium on missionaries from outside Africa has not proved an acceptable way of developing the authenticity for which African Christians yearn. Denominational and other loyalties are too firmly entrenched to be dislodged by mere fiat. This has meant that traditional theological puzzles continue to go unexamined. The hope is that as politicians succeed in weaning Africa away from the dependent mentality of a colonized people theologians will succeed in stimulating the Christian people to a creative way of talking about God in Africa. The titles of books like *African Theology en Route* (Appiah-Kubi and Torres 1979) and *Towards an African Theology* (Pobee 1979) are indicative of how far the expression of Christian theology in Africa still has to go. But the task has begun.

Christians in Africa must deal with the gap between "Christianity preached" and "Christianity lived." They must deal with racism among children of One God and disciples of the One Christ, with the exploitation and dehumanization of the sister and brother for whom Christ died. These anomalies do not escape the notice of the Muslim neighbor or the traditionalist relative. We have to face these questions: What does Christianity offer that the natural religion of our peoples does not offer? Why should an African who leaves the traditional religion become a Christian rather than a Muslim? We African Christians have only begun to probe and discuss these issues.

We who are involved in the theological enterprise in Africa must also take a critical look at the churches' stance vis-à-vis the political, economic, and social changes around us. We are duty-bound to call attention to the theological roots of the Christian role in humanization and in the struggle for justice and peace. These are universal issues, of course, for it is not only in Africa that "Christianity lived" does not measure up to "Christianity preached."

Even if we Christians in Africa could remain unmoved by contemporary events, others would demand of us an expression of hope. Ram Desai's warning in *Christianity in Africa as Seen by Africans* (1962) about "Christianity in danger" is relevant. It is not that Christianity is about to disappear from Africa. The danger is a more subtle one: it is the danger of Christianity becoming established, respectable, coopted. The ambiguous nature of missionary Christianity is slowly giving way to indigenized forms that may show an unawareness of social questions, a virtual refusal to struggle with making traditional Christian dogmas meaningful. The symbols of the faith may gradually become mere talismans and hollow incantations. Questions that were raised by the first hearers of Christianity still hang unanswered in the air: Why is the relationship of the African with the "living-dead" any more idolatrous than the observance of All Souls Day and All Saints Day? Why does the cultural and economic need for polygamy continue to confound Christian theologians and pastors? The concepts of individual choice, individuality, personhood, and communal life need to be reappraised theologically; the theology of "being chosen" and the idea of hope for a better future can no longer remain unexplored.

Any theology that hopes to be relevant will have to take into account the theological presuppositions that underlie the African worldview and social organization. African Christian theologians must come to grips with the attitudes of the church toward African social institutions in order to face the scandal of the divisions and competition within the church, as "original tribalism" is being replaced by the Christian "tribes"—Anglicans, Methodists, Roman Catholics, Baptists. Even those Africans who (like Ephraim Amu) have found "Christianity to be the best and only religion worth having" have to explain: "I do not mean Christianity as I see it in Europe but Christianity according to Jesus Christ" (Desai 1962,78). It is with this religion of Jesus that African theologians are concerned. Our salvation as Africans lies in achieving unity in our diversity and in being thankful for the gift the "other" brings.

THE ESSAYS

I have divided the material in this book into two parts: (1) Theology in Africa: Past and Present, and (2) Themes in African Theology.

Part 1 deals first with the dominant theologies of our churches, past and present, beginning with the early Christians in North Africa, Egypt, Nubia, and Ethiopia. Next I consider the modern missionary movement, which is mainly Euro-American, and is based on an imperialistic interpretation of "being sent" on mission. This missionary movement resulted in world confessional families, which parallel the transnational corporations we all know so well. I then take up sources and variants of theological insights, including those modern dogmaticians who plead the "oneness" of theology as well as those who try to be "local" and liberative. I have limited my examples to the West African experience; hence only passing references are made to black theology.

In Part 2 I introduce theological themes that I believe urgently need consideration if Africa is ever to say: "It is no longer because of your words that we believe, for we have heard for ourselves, and we know that this is indeed the Savior of the World" (Jn 4:42). Here I articulate my struggles with some aspects of Christian dogmatics as I have understood them, and theologize from my experience of Africa, Christianity, and Christian theology. Since this is an account of my faith and hope, I have deliberately kept to a minimum the theological debates that are common in many theological discourses. These essays contain my insights into traditional doctrines (creation, covenant, salvation, the Godhead, and doctrines related to Christian anthropology) and touch on ecclesiological and sacramental issues.

The mutual challenge of Christianity and life as lived day by day is being sharply felt in Africa. Here the political and economic links with "Christian" Europe and North America, the presence and activities of peoples of modern ideologies and of those of "other faiths" (especially Islam and the religious ideas and practices that emanate from it as well as those that undergird the primal worldviews of Africans) claim the attention of the Christian theologian. The worldview by which Africans live is not limited to the Christian worldview.

African leaders are struggling to hammer out ideologies; it is evident that we do not have a uniform foundation on which to build our new nations. Fluctuating, indeed often conflicting, ideological presuppositions form the base of the administration of these nations. Even the principles that once held individual ethnic groups together are lacking since our nations are made up of a multiplicity of ethnic groups. One thing, however, is clear: all who aspire to active involvement in this creative phase of African affairs must take Africa's cultural heritage seriously. In the academic world in Africa, scholars are already turning up the underside of Africa's history. The rural and the oral are now recognized as valuable sources of learning, and traditions are analyzed closely for their contribution to Africa's well-being.

If Christianity is to have a part in this reshaping of Africa, Christian theology too must respect and learn to tap Africa's "hidden" resources. In these pages I signal my willingness to share in this process.

I

CHRISTIANITY IN AFRICA: PAST AND PRESENT

1

Early Christian Theology in Africa

BACKGROUND

Missionaries from Alexandria were to be found in Ethiopia by the middle of the fourth century (Latourette 1955, 104, 17–321). By the end of that century several important dioceses had been established along the Mediterranean coast of Africa. By the end of the fifth century, Christians lived all along the Mediterranean coast of Africa in what are today the nations of Morocco, Algeria, Tunisia, Libya, and United Arab Republic (Egypt); Christianity also had moved up the Nile to Ethiopia and part of Sudan (Nubia). The Coptic church of Egypt was established by Saint Mark in Alexandria (Jerome, *Epistles* CLVI 1:1, 5–7). By the sixth century two interpretations of the faith were vying for a place in Nubia. This was happening at a time when most northern Europeans were still practicing their primal religions.

This first phase of the Christianization of Africa came to an end with the coming of Islam in the seventh century to most of what were then Christian lands. The churches of Egypt and Ethiopia survived through a series of intricate politico-religious diplomatic negotiations (Butcher 1897; Evett; 1948 Atiya). (Until the advent of the modern ecumenical movement—inaugurated formally in Amsterdam in 1948—these churches were isolated from churches in the rest of Africa.) Christianity in Nubia was slowly replaced by Islam over a period of a thousand years. Archaeological evidence is all that remains of the Christianity of that period. I believe that

Christianity failed to survive in Nubia partly because the church there had not developed a relevant theology.

This ancient Christianity in northern Africa did not send messengers of the good news to Africa south of the Sahara. The second phase of the christianization of Africa, affecting Africa south of the Sahara, was instead initiated by Latin Christians of Portugal with the blessing of a papal concordat. The Christianity of this phase did not put down strong roots on the West African coast, in the Congo estuary, Angola, and Lower Zambesi, and after two hundred years there Christianity simply decayed along with Portuguese power (Latourette 1955, 926–927).

The third phase of Africa's Christianization began in the eighteenth century, but it was not until the expansion of European trade and colonialism in the nineteenth century that the spectacular expansion of Christianity began. This third phase earned Africa the designation "mission field"; Christians in Africa were said to be from the mission churches, the younger churches, the daughter churches. The third phase too has come to an end.

Like most schemes, this one, which outlines the three phases of Africa's Christianization, is not as neat as it first appears, and deserves further theological explanation. Since it is meaningless to speak about theology without an event, I will begin with some critical points in the life of early African Christianity and examine what the Christians of that time made of them theologically.

Colonization of North Africa

The three-tiered society of Roman Africa (Tunisia and Algeria) came about as a result of two waves of colonization—first the Phoenicians from Tyre and Sidon and then the Romans. The later arrivals, the Romans, held political power and represented imperial might and authority. They were secure economically and their language was the language of commerce and education. To be properly integrated one had to be latinized. Several Phoenicians (Punics, Carthaginians) and indigenous Berbers latinized their names. This suggests the extent of the colonial power of Rome. The descendants of the Roman conquerors, an urban elite, abandoned their native gods and adopted Christianity.

The Phoenicians, who had built the city of Carthage and lost it to Rome, took second place in the social stratification. Economically they retained a fair amount of power because they continued to be involved in agriculture and commerce. Some of them became Christian but they converted more slowly than did the Romans, perhaps because their god Moloch was more alive to them. Those who became Christian did not seem to have held leadership in the church, and few Christian writings in the Punic language have been discovered.

The Berbers, the indigenous population, had lost whatever political power they once held to the colonizers; they were on the fringes of the foreign economy introduced by the Romans and worked as laborers in the cornfields and olive groves belonging to the invaders, or remained nomads, stubbornly maintaining their independence. Some became Christians and demonstrated their unbroken spirit through their interpretation of the Christian religion.

The Western version of the history of the Berbers is today challenged by both Africans and Western scholars (Frend 1952; Stevenson 1975, 303–331; Ilevbare 1980). Contrary to the popular picture presented, the Berbers were no more barbaric in defense of their natural heritage than were the Romans in seizing it. Neither did the Arian Vandals (A.D. 429–530) perpetrate more vandalism in the area than that inflicted on life and property by the Roman Byzantine overlords and their military expeditions. These encounters did not bring about any growth in Christianity, as the indigenous people (Berbers or Moors) could not wholeheartedly accept the religion of the conquerors, the Romano-Africans. The religion of "slave masters" and conquerors, even when it is adopted by their subjects, takes on a different meaning and significance for them.

Church and State

Members of all three strata of the society of Roman Africa who became Christians were at best ambivalent toward Roman culture and imperial power; generally their attitude was negative. They were hostile to Roman institutions; they refused to join in the imperial cult (which included sacrifices); they refused to take part in games, to accept municipal appointments, even to read non-Christian literature. By the time of Cyprian (the middle of the third century) acceptance of Christ implied a rejection of Greco-Roman culture. The Roman presence was rejected to the extent that some considered Roman officials and magistrates to be the personification of the power of evil. Yet Augustine, the great theologian, did not hesitate to make use of the imperial power in order to suppress an indigenous Christianity. He even used a parable to justify his action—the parable of the great feast: "Compel them to come in" (Lk 14:23).

Of course, the times had changed: the imperial policy of Tertullian's days (197–225) and the intolerable sufferings of the Cyprianic period (248–251) had given way to the Constantinian era. When Augustine was combating Donatism, the emperors were Christian. Yet within the Christian community there was a split. The imperial favor shown the one half confirmed the other half in its intransigence. What has the emperor to do with the church? the disfavored group asked (Frend 1975, chap. 16).

THEOLOGIES IN THE FIRST PHASE OF CHRISTIANITY

The North African church was never truly monolithic. In the middle of the third century Carthage had three rival bishops: Maximum (Novatian party); Fortunatus (schismatic); and Cyprian (Catholic orthodox). They all saw themselves as belonging to the one church, but there was an underlying debate as to where this church was located. There existed both what one might call the "Church of the Holy Spirit" and a "Catholic Church," that is, one with a universalist outlook.

In the days of Tertullian (the first quarter of the third century), the Church of the Holy Spirit was openly hostile to the world and emphasized charisma over an ordered episcopate. The Montanists, who emphasized the presence of the Holy Spirit, found support here (Stevenson 1963, 107–114, 187). Tertullian (himself once a Montanist) and others taught that the church was not a school for salvation but a community of saints awaiting the end of the world, which was soon to happen (Harnack, 108–112; Tertullian, *De Pudicitia*). The Holy Spirit was believed to be in the whole Christian community; this belief combined with the teaching that a Christian who sinned was by definition no longer a Christian. The opposing view (which later became Catholic orthodoxy) was a more subtle and dialectical approach introduced by Cyprian and later perfected by Augustine.

Popular Christianity did not seem to have been altogether on the side of the theologians who became the church dogmaticians. It was in fact more on the side of those whose views were suppressed. The Montanists of Tertullian's day and the Novatians of Cyprian's (in the third century) were eventually disowned by the consensus of "universal Christianity." The long history of the Donatist controversy (fourth century) surrounding the validity and efficiency of the sacraments was brought to an end with the suppression of Donatism by the imperial might called in by Augustine after his theological arguments had failed to persuade. The history of Christianity in Africa does not substantiate the concept of a uniform or monolithic African theology in the past or present.

I do not intend to disown Augustine, a true son of Africa. I only suggest that the truly African spirit apparent in all these controversies was that manifested by the Montanists and the Donatists. When Donatism was suppressed, the people, mostly the indigenous Berbers, were only too happy to side with Allah's troops and against Yahweh's.

The Religious Context

The pre-Christian, primal religions of the North Africans centered around the spirits of natural objects, deities from Phoenicia, and the gods of the Roman pantheon. All three tended toward monotheism in their recognition of Saturn (the spirit of the sun), corresponding to a Supreme God. All agreed that the worship of the Supreme God entailed total submission to that God here and now, judgment in the hereafter, and a literal rising of the bodies of those who had died. Religious practices included sacrifice—when Baal Haamon-Moloch demanded your children, you gave them up. Exorcism and the use of talismans have been reported.

With the arrival of Christianity some simply added Jehovah and his son Jesus to the pantheon; others identified Jehovah with Saturn. Some professing Christians held syncretistic views: "I go to idols, I consult seers and magicians but I do not abandon God's church" (Frend 1952, 103). From such a diverse background one would expect a variety of theological insights from Christians. One insight commonly predominated: the willingness to die for one's beliefs.

The Church of the Martyrs

Faced with persecution, the church chose martyrdom. Martyrdom's theological base was absolute loyalty to God, which made participation in the imperial cult unthinkable. Traditional rigorous attitudes relating to the demands of the gods were reinforced by many biblical statements:

> As for those people who were once brought into the light, and tasted the gift from heaven, and received a share of the Holy Spirit, and appreciated the good message of God and the powers of the world to come, and yet in spite of this have fallen away—it is impossible for them to be renewed a second time. They cannot be repentant if they have willfully crucified the Son of God and openly mocked him [Hb 6:4-6].

> If, after we have been given knowledge of the truth, we should deliberately commit any sins, then there is no longer any sacrifice for them [Hb 10:26; see also 12:17].

> You will be hated by all men on account of my name; but the man who stands firm to the end will be saved [Mk 13:13].

> Do not be afraid of those who kill the body. . . . but the man who disowns me in the presence of men will be disowned in the presence of God's angels [Lk 12:4, 9].

It is no wonder then that the first time the North African church appears in the written records of Christianity it is to name its martyrs: twelve Berber Christians who had refused to swear by the "Lord our Emperor" were dispatched to meet their Lord. In the theology of the North African church, to reject these Roman rites was to gain instant admission to heaven (Acts Scilli 5). At the point of death, the Christians shouted *Hodie martyres in coelis sumus* (Stevenson 1975, 41-43). From the same North African church come the stories of Perpetua and Felicitas and the account of the martyrdom of Cyprian. From the North African church come statements of faith such as "a good purpose which knows God cannot be altered" (Stevenson 1975, 227), and "when the right is so clear there is nothing to consider" (42).

These Christians were sure that it was better to die than to act contrary to their faith. But the choice was not always so clear. Cyprian, during the Decian persecution, used Scripture to explain a different response to persecution. He went into hiding in order to be available to guide the church (Stevenson 1975, 235–236).

If they persecute you in one town, take refuge in the next; and if they persecute you in that, take refuge in another. I tell you solemnly, you will not have gone the round of the towns of Israel before the Son of Man comes [Mt 10:23].

Cyprian tells us of others who did not follow the line of absolute loyalty but simply complied with the authorities in order to save their own necks. (During Diocletian's persecution of Christians a state official did report that "all Africans had sacrificed" [Frend 1952, 501]). One could argue that running away is better than staying to perjure oneself. Nevertheless, Cyprian incurred the anger of those who stayed. He escaped death only because the persecution came to an end with the death of the Roman emperor Decius (A.D. 251).

The debate among Christians that followed the period of persecution by Decius resulted in Cyprian's ecclesiology, which held that outside the church there is no salvation. Cyprian also brought to North African Christians the insights that no one should be excluded from the sacrament of penance and that the church was empowered to forgive any sin, including the sin of apostasy.

All this was no armchair preaching; it was theology—a struggle to understand what obedience to Christ meant in particular circumstances. We should note also that the theological task was the struggle of the whole Christian community and not simply that of Christian leaders like Cyprian, Fortunatus, and Maximus.

Theology in Deeds

The theology of the North African church was also expressed in deeds other than martyrdom. When a plague broke out in A.D. 252, Cyprian led the Christians not only in prayer but also in practical ministry to the sick, the dying, and the dead. Those they served were not all members of the Christian community (Stevenson 1975, 245–246). Such a ministry must have cost some Christians their lives. Under the leadership of Cyprian, Christians collected relief funds and organized the ransom of persons who had been taken prisoner during a political revolt.

We are told that these practical activities brought many people to a recognition of the lordship of Christ. The response of the Christians to martyrdom, plague, and captivity was clearly based on belief in a God who demanded loyalty, who stood for wholeness of body and spirit, and who expected people to work for the realization of this wholeness. Others were challenged by this Christian view of reality and were themselves forced to take a stand.

The Theology of the Donatist Wing of the Church

The persecution and eventual suppression of Donatism, an indigenous African Christianity, enabled Islam to conquer the area now known as Mauritania, Morocco, Tunisia, Algeria, and Libya. With the coming of Islam, the "expatriate population," that is, the descendants of the Romans, simply fled back to Europe pursued by the Arabs, who were aided by the indigenous Berbers. Why should Christian Berbers aid Arab Moslems, or were they not "really" Christian?

In the forty years between the persecutions of Valerius and Diocletian (known as the "Little Peace"), North Africa became one of the most Christian areas of the Roman Empire. The national deity lost popularity, but the strict discipline that went with the national religion remained and reinforced the absolute loyalty to Christ learned from Christian writings.

The Diocletian edicts (A.D. 303–305) resulted in the burning of the Christian scriptures and the demolishing of Christian churches in North Africa. Many Christians complied with the imperial demand to hand over Christian literature to destruction. Indirectly, this set off the Donatist movement, which rocked the church well into the sixth century. The story goes that certain Christians objected to the election of a bishop of Carthage. They charged that his consecration at the hands of Felix, bishop of Aptunga, was invalid because Felix had handed over sacred books and relics to the civil authorities. These Christians believed that only those living a blameless life could belong in the church. Large areas came under the Donatist movement, which was popular with the indigenous Berbers. (The Donatists had supported the Berber revolts.)

The Donatists saw themselves as the Church of the Confessors, intolerant of backsliders, over against the Catholics, whom they accused of compromising with imperial power. Both sides claimed Cyprian as their ecclesiological authority. This controversy indirectly brought about the separation of church and state, an idea now accepted by Western civilization. Augustine argued against the Donatists and drove them underground. Together with the Catholics, the Donatists suffered persecution at the hands of the Germanic Arians (another Christian group). By A.D. 523 the "lost" territory was again under Roman rule, but not long afterwards (A.D. 647) the Moslem-Arabs overcame the ruling class made up of Catholic Christians. The Berbers resisted the Arabs briefly but in A.D. 703 they went over en masse to Islam, which made them more welcome than Christianity had ever done.

Why did the Berbers feel more at home with Islam than with Christianity? My reading of the situation is that, great as Cyprian and Augustine were, their theology did not truly reflect the spirituality of the Berbers. To the Berbers, sin (in this case apostasy) was contagious and should not be trifled with. The church is de facto holy, that is, it is made up of good women and men. One sees the struggle to resolve this issue in Augustine's theology as worked out in the *City of God*. The Donatist position on the sacraments was in tune with their ecclesiology. How are people to confer the gift of the Holy Spirit through their ministration if they themselves do not possess it or rather are not possessed by it? Today of course we are all relieved because we can follow Optatus of Melevis (ca. A.D. 365) (see Stevenson 1975, 404) and believe that the efficacy of the sacraments derives from God and not from the person who administers them and that the holiness of the church does not depend on the holiness of its members (Frend 1952, 21, 135, 324). The fact remains that Donatism was repressed at the expense of an indigenous insight into Christian belief.

From this African Christianity one learns several things.

1. The gospel has to be dynamically related to a people's "primal religion" if they are to be brought to Christ. Today's primal religions may not be the worship of gods but other more immediate concerns—an ideology, physical comfort, self-esteem, or perhaps a vision of what life on earth could be.

2. A theology that will sustain a people's religion and piety will probably not be one produced by an intellectual elite or a hierarchi-

cal power, but one that is born from the people's experience of God-in-action. A relevant theology for me is one built upon the understanding of faith that one finds among the people even before the intellectual elite has begun to cast it in scientific language.

3. In the rural areas of North Africa the people's religion had run parallel with Christianity; most Christians were really adherents of some kind of a transformed version of their primal religion rather than converts who completely adopted a new religion. Clearly, ideas from traditional religions either passed into or reinforced the Judeo-Christian ideas. The emphasis on asceticism and martyrdom gave Christianity a strong expiatory character. Ritual fasts and penance were advocated. Cyprian for instance taught that "by repentance God is appeased." A covenant relationship with God meant that performing the correct ritual brought about the desired effect. Prayer followed strictly formulated patterns. Exorcism was common and the symbols of the cross and the fish were often used. From the time of Tertullian to the time of Augustine (A.D. 200–400) the Christianity preached in North Africa emphasized fear more than love. Tertullian taught that "fear is the foundation of salvation." Augustine elaborated: "God orders man to love him and threatens deep miseries if he does not do so."

The theology that triumphed was the one supported by the European allies of Augustine. Christian Berbers, the few who did not go over to Islam, fled into the mountains. There is evidence of about forty episcopal sees in North Africa during the ninth century. The Muslim rulers of the time allowed them to exist as long as they paid tribute. Their existence was, however, an ideological embarrassment to Rome. These North African sees had been influenced by Arabic culture. Celibacy was no virtue to them. They called their bishops *Calif*. The only signs of Christianity left among the Berbers were the use of the cross as an ornament and the words *Mesi* (a name for God) and *angelous* (angel) (Bovill 1933, 115–116, 24).

Early Theology of the Nile Basin

Egypt. The Nile Basin[1] of Egypt offered the Roman world the cult of Isis and Osiris. From that cult came the expectation of the resurrection of the body, which was the Egyptian reason for embalming the dead. Osiris ("waters of the Nile") died yearly and yearly was raised by the weeping of Isis. The gospel of a real man who died and rose again was easily accepted here. Osiris was a god; this man too was God. The gratitude shown to Isis was passed on to Mary. Egypt, Ethiopia, and Nubia all held the *Theotokos* (Mother of God) doctrine in high esteem and have elaborate mariologies. The one nature (divine-human) of the Christ was so real to them that they were prepared to reject the Chalcedonian formulation of the nature of the Christ.[2]

The mariology of Orthodox Christianity put Christian women on pedestals and viewed them as "the neck that turns the head," but their roles were fixed and could not be modified even by individual talents. Ethiopian monks put their monasteries in the far recesses of their mountainous country partly to isolate themselves from women.

The theological heritage here is clear: as Isis brought life back to Osiris so Mary gave life to the son of God. The theological implications of this for women and for the church are tremendous.

Isis-based theology is not the only carry-over from Egyptian primal religion to Christianity. The river Nile provided the people with other religious experiences. Prayers beseeched its rise and fall; the floods provided the church with a rhythm for its religious calendar. Circumcision, a custom in Egypt, was proscribed by other Christian communities but continued in Egypt. Several other pre-Christian customs—burial rites, for example—are still extant (Latourette 1944, 20–28; see also CMS, 36). The theologies of Origen and Athanasius have their roots in Egypt—Coptic monks once gave refuge to Athanasius. The interaction of faiths and philosophies in Alexandria helped to shape Christian theology toward the formula of Nicaea. By the sixth century we see a distinctly Coptic Christianity, which is informed by its devotion to Mary, the *Theotokos*.

Suddenly formal theological debates and growth stopped. The church survived through the strength of its ritual as Islam bore down on it. The church concentrated on its seven sacraments; it revered its icons of Mary, Mark, and other saints; it continued to read the Bible in the Coptic language long after the words had lost their meaning to the rank and file and the time given over to its ritual lengthened so the people could take refuge in a secure place.

Ethiopia. Athanasius sent the first mission to Ethiopia. The Abunas, the patriarchs of the Ethiopian Orthodox Church, were appointed from Egypt and held the theology of the mother church. But the political context was different from that of Egypt, and so a different theological base for church-state relations was formed. The thirteenth-century Armenian writer Abu Salih wrote:

> All the Kings of Abyssinia are priests, and celebrate the liturgy within the Sanctuary as long as they reign without slaying a man with their own hands [Evett 1895, 286].

With the coming of Islam, Christianity was protected by the power of the government, not by the strength of its theology. In the early days it had taken the path of inculturation, identified local trinities with the Christian Trinity, turned traditional temples into Christian churches, and maintained magical practices that came from the primal religions. Most important, the nation and the church were one; there was no dichotomy of secular and sacred. The emperor was *pontifex maximus*, intermediary between church and state. The Ethiopians did not say he was divine (although in recent times some Africans divinized Haile Selassie when he was alive).

It is noteworthy that apotheosis and divine kingship are integral to the primal worldviews of Africa. Ethiopian Christianity was an indigenized religion; of the remembered traditional religions, some were related to Judaism, while others had been absorbed into Christianity. But this indigenization was not theologized, and the close relationship of church and state meant that no prophetic voice developed. There was no independent Christian opinion on national life. Like the churches in Europe and America, the Ethiopian church condoned slavery; it even owned slaves (Westermann 1935, 112). But that church, because it was rooted in the soil of Ethiopia, survived. It continues to survive today's attacks from Western Christianity and European ideologies.

Nubia. Christianity in medieval Nubia could be described as the religion of the urbanized and upper classes that was gradually absorbed into Islam through intermarriage. It is difficult to reconstruct the faith by which the ordinary, rural Nubian lived. The Bible was introduced in Nubia in A.D. 540, but how many could read?

The Nubians had their own liturgy and maintained close contact with Egypt until Islam and the Funj (a nomadic people that raided southern Nubia) made that impossible. They made pilgrimages and developed monasticism. Their kings built many churches and monasteries. The Nubian church had a well-organized catechesis. Because of their thorough grounding in Christian doctrine, the population remained Christian throughout the period of Muslim rule in the fourteenth century.

What exactly did Nubian Christianity teach? It could simply have transmitted Christian practices. Some Sudanese today who are not Christians do baptize their children; it is simply part of their culture to do so (Anderson 1963, 25). Christian-Muslim dialogue of today could benefit from Nubian studies, not least on the theological level, when all the scrolls unearthed have been deciphered.

What we do know today about Nubian Christianity of the period from A.D. 540 to 1500 suggests that it bore characteristics similar to colonial Christianity in Africa of the 1940s and 1950s: (1) foreign leadership was appointed by the patriarch of Egypt (Alexandria); (2) books were imported and translated; and (3) its dependence on the outside resulted in the church being "starved" to death when the Muslims succeeded in isolating Nubia from Egypt. The Nubian church had no local resources on which to depend. If one had called a theological consultation in the eleventh century, Nubia would have echoed the theology of the Coptic Church.

Today we still have African theologians whose insights are those of their mainline counterparts in Tübingen or Birmingham; we have pastors of African flocks whose ecclesiastical orders follow those of their mentors. If these are positions they have reasoned out for themselves, then there is hope; if not, then we should remember that Christianity in Nubia succumbed to Islam after a thousand years. Churches in many parts of Africa are only celebrating centenaries.

Let me make a few observations.

1. Nile Basin Christianity survived Islamization to the degree that it was rooted in the culture of the people.

2. Where there is no indigenous leadership, a converting faith, such as Christianity, cannot hope to take root (see examples of Nubia and North Africa above).

3. A balance between the local and the universal expression of

Christianity is necessary. It was the insistence that the universal church should assent to a universally formulated creed that broke the spirit of the early church in Africa and gave Islam its chance.

4. The Catholics of North Africa and the Melkites of Egypt would in today's Africa be labeled as people with a "colonial mentality" or "Bwana mentality," their teaching imbued by "missionary theology." Indigenous churches holding to the apron strings of Euro-American mothers will never mature.

5. An indigenous church will have an irrelevant theology if only its leadership, liturgy, and vestments are affected by the process of contextualization and if it remains uninvolved in the sociopolitical realities of its members and of the continent in which it seeks to reflect Christ.

6. It is possible to retain the forms and symbols of Christianity without affecting personal or national life. The forms and practices of a religion can survive the vicissitudes of persecution, but for a religion to really make a difference in the daily lives of people its theological foundations must be strong and must be laid in and by the people.

7. Finally, I note the interrelatedness of theology, nationalism, and socioeconomic matters. The Donatist church won the nationalistic Berbers; nationalism fueled the Chalcedonian debate; Christianity in Ethiopia was domesticated by nationalism and disappeared from Nubia when political power gradually passed into Muslim hands. African theology today cannot avoid elements of nationalism. After all, *Idan si ho a na posu ban simu*, "The altar survives if the house stands."

Some theologians in Africa specialize in "theologizing" the political stance of their governments. They were in Ghana during the heyday of the Nkrumah administration. Some white Christians of South Africa have theological, "biblically based" arguments geared to making sinners of black Christians of Africa if they refuse the white yoke.

There must be some way of distinguishing nationalism and selfhood from a theology that is contextual. We must look to the guidance of Christ. That guidance will make our contextual theology relevant universally. If it is true to Christ it will bring judgment on the same factors everywhere and will call forth commitment to the kingdom of God that Jesus came to announce.

2

The Modern Missionary Movement and Christian Dogma in Africa

BACKGROUND: "CHRISTIANIZING" AFRICA

The history of the modern missionary movement in Africa begins with Europeans' attempts to "re-Christianize" or "Christianize" various areas of northern Africa, some of which had been ancient strongholds of Christianity. The Franciscans and Dominicans began missionary work (Raymond Lull in the thirteenth century is an example) in Mediterranean Africa; the Portuguese began evangelizing along the Gold Coast in 1471; there was an attempt to Latinize the Ethiopian church in the sixteenth century. The Latin church operated in northern Africa a sort of reformed crusade. It transplanted the Roman rites in Africa. Later, large numbers of Protestants were infused into this missionary endeavor. In England and America the evangelical movement of the early eighteenth century awakened many Christians to the implications of bearing the name of Christ. This awakening particularly informed the Protestant endeavors. Neither the Latin nor the Protestant effort achieved spectacular results. They exhibited only spectacular insensitivity.

Ethiopia

In 1541 the Portuguese helped the Ethiopians to drive the Muslims away. By 1600, Portuguese priests were on Ethiopian soil finding endless fault with the Ethiopian church: the priests were married, the church did not recognize the pope as head of the universal church. The Roman Catholic mission at one time ordered drastic reforms, rebaptizing people and reconsecrating churches and priests. The Roman Catholics rebuilt altars, replaced *Ge'ez* (the liturgical language of the Ethiopian Orthodox Church) with Latin and installed a Portuguese Abuna (patriarch) in the place of the Egyptian one. It is one more irony of the dialogue between indigenous and imperialist Christianity that the Ethiopians sought the help of Muslims along the coast of the Red Sea to prevent Europeans from entering Ethiopia (Mikre-Selassie 1976).

In 1896 Italian troops attempting to enter Ethiopia were driven back. Their brief occupation of the country (1936–1941) was the only formal colonialism that Ethiopia ever suffered. When the Protestants, in the form of the Church Missionary Society (CMS), came to Ethiopia, they reported that "Abyssinia possesses a Christian Church, the most corrupt and superstitious in the world," and they proceeded to lay plans to turn these Christians into Anglican Christians (CMS 1899, 44–45).

Egypt and Nubia

Protestantism came to Egypt in the person of John Hogg, a Presbyterian. His aim there was to reform the Coptic Church. He was rebuffed by the patriarch, who told Hogg: "We had the Gospel before America was born." The Presbyterians were expelled. Some younger Copts caught Hogg's vision of a Christianity without icons, and a small Western-style Christianity took shape in the midst of the ancient Egyptian Church (Anderson 1963, 18–19).

The Verona Missionaries (RCM) set for themselves the task of rehabilitating Nubia. Their first missionaries arrived in Khartoum in 1820. Half of them perished; the other half went home. In 1858 Daniele Comboni developed his "Win Africa by Africans" policy, went to the slave market in Cairo, bought slaves, Christianized them, and sent them to Sudan (*National Greater News* 1981; see also Gilli 1977, 62).

Once more two versions of Christianity met in Khartoum. The Khartoum government returned to the "Win Africa by Africans" policy after the civil war that ravaged the country in the 1960s. That policy has been modified again, and European missionaries are now allowed entry into Sudan.

Conflicts between ancient Christianity and Western versions of Christianity may be illustrated by analogous events in Asia. In India the liturgical books of the Syrian Church (the Malabar rites of the Mar Toma Church) were collected and burned by Western Christians. Attempts to westernize were a source of agony to those churches, and the insensitivity with which westernization was promoted is still fresh in their collective memory (Latourette 1955, 315 316).

West Africa

Europe's attention turned from northern Africa and the Nile Basin to West Africa after the Portuguese adventurers brought gold and slaves back to Europe. The conversion of Africans to Christianity was one of the motives behind those adventures and "even slave-raiding and slave-trading were seriously regarded as acts of Christian charity, because they seemed to be the only means by which the salvation of heathen souls could be effected" (Westermann 1935, 142).

By the time the Protestant nations joined the hunt for souls, slaves, and earthly treasure, nothing remained of the Latin efforts at Christianization in West Africa. They described the whole region as an area "where barbarity and cannibalism reigned undisturbed" and spoke of South Africa of the mid-nineteenth century as "the hardest of all fields, the borderlands of native barbarism and European civilization." What these missionaries saw in Africa was "the superstitious barbarism of Africa . . . who seeks to appease the evil spirit" (CMS 1899, 167).

THE MISSIONARIES TO AFRICA

Roman Catholics, Anglicans, Presbyterians, Methodists, Baptists, and Mormons—all were missionaries to Africa. For Africans one thing was clear: the missionary was a foreigner. Missionaries were mostly of a different human-type (call it a race). Even when the missionaries were black, they were usually strangers to the local language, customs, and culture. These were difficult people to accommodate. Not even Philip Quaque, "the first of any non-European race since the Reformation to receive Anglican orders" (CMS 1899, 4), was accounted an authentic African even by his own people.

From the point of view of background and religious convictions, most of the missionaries were products of the eighteenth-century evangelical awakening. They were "men who had experienced the Grace of God in their own hearts and lives" and were (by that fact alone) "qualified to proclaim the messages of that grace to others" (CMS 1899, 14).

One of the five missionary principles laid down by John Venn—a founding member of the Society for Missions to Africa and the East, which became the Church Missionary Society for Africa and the East (CMS)—was that "a missionary should have heaven in his heart and tread the world under his foot," adding that "only God can raise such men" (CMS 1899, 15). The Society for Missions to Africa and the East adjudged that "men not fitted for English ordination might yet prove good missionaries to savages rude and illiterate" (Ibid., 17, 19, 77–78, 115, 147–149). Similar descriptions of missionaries can be found in many missionary archives. They were probably intended (even though not maliciously) to belittle the recipient of the mission, but what they succeeded in doing was to convince African intellectuals that only the second-rate and the ne'er-do-well found their way into colonial and missionary service. We know it is not so in every case, but it is an unfortunate legacy all the same. Newman and others saw the danger early enough, but evangelical zeal brushed their legitimate fears aside, and people of dubious intelligence and integrity were launched upon the unsuspecting "savages" of Africa south of the Sahara.

These were the first teachers of Christian dogmatics to the African. Those the CMS sent to the Preparatory Institute of Islington and not to Durham were described as "young men of promise but not of superior education." Later the social class of the missionary was at issue. This is seen in the Keswick Letter of 1890. This letter advocated moving forward in the missionary enterprise and included a plea that "efforts be made to enlist and train men and women of humbler social position, though not otherwise inferior" (Hewitt 1910–1942, 1:459). By 1937, J. H. Oldham and others had convinced the Protestants that reason too was a gift from God. J. H. Oldham said: "The task of the missionary is to communicate a life, and his training must be related to his capacity to grow, to learn and to live in fellowship with others" (ibid.).

That Europeans suffered in Africa, made sacrifices, and showed dedication and heroism is a fact apart from all the exaggerations of their own accounts and the hagiographies of their admirers. But so did the rarely named African collaborators who carried the missionaries on their backs and in hammocks and who interpreted for them. What comes through to the African who reads the history of the missionary efforts of Europeans in Africa is the ethnocentricity of the account. It was an exercise in cultural occupation. In fact missionary accounts often speak of "occupying" or "reoccupying" towns. The missionaries gave people names that only the Europeans could pronounce "correctly" because they found African names too difficult to say, or too heathen to enter into their Book of Life, which their God kept in their heaven.

When I was growing up in the 1940s and the 1950s with missionaries, I did not see the missionaries' "capacity to live in fellowship with others" unless the "others" meant other Europeans. If anything, the isolation of the missionaries from the people was more noticeable even than that of the British administrators. I suppose at that time the zeal to make us (Africans) in their (European) image that we might enter heaven was flagging; they certainly were not going to live like us. There were exceptions, and they are the ones we still appreciate. We say of them that "they tried."

Missionaries to Africa even today are not prepared to be in partnership with the African. What the CMS Missionaries said about the people they met in 1869 still operates for some Euro-American missionaries:

Thus we have gone round the world
We have seen the proud Brahman
The fanatical Mussulman,
The self-satisfied Buddhist—
The Superstitious barbarian of Africa or the South Seas
who seeks to appease the evil spirits;
The highly educated Hindu
and the ignorant black fellow of Australia;
and we have found that in two very deep senses
there is no difference.

All alike belong to the sinful and ruined family of man.
The same Lord over all is rich unto all who call him.
There is One Race, One Revelation and One Redeemer
                                            [CMS 1899, 171].

This was the faith preached but hardly ever lived.

THE MARGINALIZED OF AFRICA

For the African theologian, African converts were not superstitious barbarians; they were people with a history and events the theologians needed to interpret. The first Christians of Sierra Leone and Liberia went through the indignity of being captured and sold; some actually suffered the hell of slavery. William Johnson and Henry Düring preached to "1,400 poor creatures out of a slave ship wretched in every respect" in Sierra Leone. Hardly had Johnson begun to teach them and pray for them when the Holy Spirit fell on them.

Here were a people totally ignorant, and with scarcely an idea of purity and virtue and honesty, in a few weeks and months found to know what sin is, who Christ is, how sin can be put away, how Christ can be trusted and served; found, moreover, to be quiet, devout, truthful and industrious as testified by the government officials in the colony [CMS 1899, 33-34].

Gratitude made the liberated African adopt the religion of the benefactor. Here indeed was a gospel of salvation materially demonstrated.

Not surprisingly, few records of failures to convert the Africans exist. Neither do we have much analysis of why some Africans rejected the gospel of salvation—there is a marked lack of analysis of this from the African point of view (Horton 1971, 85-108). Incidents such as the following—a conversation between Rev. Adolfus Mann (of the CMS) and Are Kakanfo Kurunmi (a Yoruba general)—are rarely recorded. The dramatist Ola Rotimi reconstructed the conversation. The dialogue begins after Reverend Mann has delivered a lengthy monologue during which he declined to sit.

Kurunmi: Hmm. Have you finished?

Rev. Mann: I have tried, Your Greatness, not to trouble you with the problems of my mission. But matters have reached a point where I feel that Your Greatness must do something to get your people to respond better to the Scriptures.

K: Have you anything more to say?

M: That is all, Your Greatness. (*Kurunmi is silent again.*) I have finished, Your Greatness.

K: It is well. I thank you. Now sit down. (*Rev. Mann sits.*) Reverend Mann, have you a father?

M: I beg your pardon?

K: Father, father—have you a father?

M: You mean . . . dead or living?

K: It does not matter. Have you ever had a father?

M: Well . . . of course . . . indeed, I . . . Yes, I had a father.

K: I don't think so.

M: I beg your pardon!

K: Reverend Mann, I don't think you ever had a father.

M: Your Greatness!

K: Oh, but it is true. If you had a father, Reverend Mann, the way you think would be different. Imagine me for a moment. I go to your country, and tell your father: "Mr. So-and-So, snub the shrines of your fathers; betray your gods." Now, Reverend Mann, how do you think your father would feel?

M: The people of Oyo have accepted the faith, and in Ibadan Reverend Hinderer is doing very well . . . the Reverend Townsend in Abeokuta, and other . . .

K: My friend, you do not answer my question. Instead you talk of Ibadan and Oyo and . . . Go on, try. Preach all you want [Rotimi 1979, 32–36].

A similar incident took place in 1876. Nana Mensah (an Asante ruler) told Picot (a Wesleyan missionary): "The Bible is for the White man, the Muslims have another book, and we the Asante have our own religion. We know and keep all God's commandments and have no need for Christianity."

For these Africans the mission was an affront and a threat. The Asante maintained that Christianity weakened and spoiled Fantiland (the area of Ghana occupied by the Fantes), making the high man the same as the low. The only reason they allowed missionaries to stay was because of their function as peacemakers when trouble brewed between the colonial and the traditional Asante powers.

It seems that the lack of theological depth in the missionary enterprise came from the failure to face the African's objections to Christianity. Some Africans took a wait-and-see stance, believing and hoping that *Ehia oburoni a ɔka Twi*, "When the white man is in a tight corner he will speak the language of the people." A benign tolerance of the religious views of others is firmly rooted in Africa; it is part of African hospitality. Nevertheless, strangers who want to be accepted and to be taken into confidence are expected to learn the ways of the natives. The Western missionaries were slow to realize that they did not have as much knowledge and feel for the African soul and style of life as they thought they had. The African was not an open book. This came as a shock with the overwhelming evidence that confessing Christ for the African had not meant a total turning away from traditional religious practices. People known to be Christians were also known to be consulting oracles. Traditional African spirituality began finally to surface and to blossom in Christian churches founded by Africans. It became evident that "I have heard" is not the same as "I accept" even though the two phrases sound alike, as indeed they actually do in Yoruba to the ears of the uninitiated.

The early successes of the missionaries caused them to draw the conclusion articulated by Diedrich Westermann:

Because the African loves what Europe offers him, he also loves Christianity, which in his eyes is the religion of the White man. . . . For them [the Africans] Christianity is the greatest gift that has come to them from beyond the seas [Westermann 1935, 28–29].

In such a euphoric situation there was little development of what could be properly described as theology. These Westerners thought that they were dealing with empty pitchers sitting in a vacant room. Thus while not too long ago Billy Graham found it necessary to say that "It is estimated there are some 40 million Africans still worshipping the old bush gods" (Desai 1962, 14), the approach continues to be "a single word will cast them out." The mission to Africa in the eyes of some missionaries is still basically the task of setting forth "in all their simplicity and fullness the great facts of sin and salvation, to the perishing African" (CMS 1899, 35).

Lesslie Newbigin, a retired bishop of the Church of South India, offered an explanation for the success of the early mission similar to that of Westermann, only it is stated with more sensitivity to the historical context of the enterprise: "A century ago the Western nations so dominated the world that most of the rest of mankind stood in awe of the white man and accepted his claim to political, cultural and religious leadership" (Newbigin 1978, 6). Unlike Billy Graham, Newbigin recognizes that this is a new era. His words also suggest that he suspects that the African's acceptance of Christianity was tentative; the African was giving the white man's religion a trial. Just as the Asantes predicted *Ehia oburoni a ɔka twi*, so the fine shade of difference between *gbo* (hear) and *gba* (accept) is being recognized by western interpreters of the African scene.

A THEOLOGY OF SOUL-SNATCHING

The missionaries to Africa had behind them the evangelical revival and were preachers of the evangelical truth: (1) human beings were dead in sin and guilty before God; (2) Christ died to save human beings from sin's penalty; (3) Christ lives to save them from sin's power; (4) only faith in Christ can give human beings Christian salvation; (5) absolute conversion of heart and life was needed by all; and (6) the Holy Spirit convicts and sanctifies human beings (CMS 1899, 5). This was the word from overseas, preached in Africa. It was a coherent story, and those who were convinced by it were converted. It had its own logic and those who argued against the basic assumptions went unrecorded, had the truth drummed even louder into their ears, and when all had failed were numbered among "those who are perishing." The mandate of the missionary was to "preach Christ and him crucified or hold your peace" (CMS 1899, 65). The spirit of the nineteenth-century missionaries is preserved in Frances Jane van Alstyne's hymn:

Rescue the perishing, care for the dying.
Snatch them in pity from sin and the grave;

Weep o'er the erring one, lift up the fallen,
Tell them of Jesus, the mighty to save.
Rescue the perishing, care for the dying;
Jesus is merciful, Jesus will save.

[Van Alstyne 1962 (1933), no. 338].

This attitude was the core of *Instructions to Missionaries*, but from time to time and depending on what controversies raged at home, doctrines like the infallibility of Scripture, the miraculous birth of Jesus, the second coming, and the gifts of the Holy Spirit would receive special mention. To tell the story of salvation the missionaries clung to the infallibility of Scripture while in their homelands some fought rationalism and theories of evolution to defend the same view of Scripture.

The Christian scheme of salvation depended on a worldview built around the creation of a good universe, the special position of human beings within this creation, the fall, the coming of the Savior, and the imminent restoration of all to primeval goodness and hence to God. Among the missionaries, of course, there were some differences of opinion. Some held that "evangelization of the world is not identical with the conversion of the world" and others wanted to see converts multiplying and churches growing. For most of the evangelicals however, evangelization, the task of missionaries, was needed and needed urgently to prepare for the second coming. Thus a sharp division between mission and church was created.

THE THEOLOGY FROM PRAXIS

Not much reasoned or systematic argument took place. There did not seem to be the need, nor were the tools for it available. All the emphasis was on proclamation. Yet one would have to agree with Kathleen Heasman, who says the evangelicals are "remembered for what they did rather than for their theology" (Heasman 1962, 15) and for the simple fact that they continued to come if only to die. Wrigley's last appeal to his people of the Wesleyan Methodist Missionary Society was to "come out to this hell, if it is only to die here" (Bartels 1965, 27). A study of martyrs and martyrdom in the church in Africa would have to include these missionaries who were Christians first and Europeans second.

The theology of the missionaries in Africa can be read from what they did. Although the European organizations that supported them insisted that their "civilizing" activities were a consequence rather than a means of proclaiming the gospel, the impression we got at the receiving end was different: schools and hospitals served as instruments for conversion. The two cannot be divorced. The missionaries were bringing salvation and "civilization" to Africa. However, their civilization was a suspect model. In 1815, while the Europeans were making their statement about proclamation and civilizing activity, there was no dearth of proclamation in Birmingham, England, and yet in that city one out of every three people was a pauper, crime was on the increase; and riots were being put down by military force (CMS 1899, 36; see also Plumb 1955). In 1851, Queen Victoria was telling the chiefs of Abeokuta that "England has become great and happy by the knowledge of the true God and Jesus Christ" at a time when the "bloodthirsty kings and warriors of Dahomey were bent on the destruction of Abeokuta" (CMS 1899, 84–88).[1]

It seems to me that salvation had been given too narrow a definition. The Bible is full of cries for salvation, culminating in the hope for the coming of the Messiah according to the Jews and the hope of his second coming according to the Christians. Salvation is still a key theme in theology in Africa. What is this salvation of the heathen soul that the missionaries wanted to effect? Since the emphasis was on souls rather than on persons, a dualism of thinking and acting informed the missionary era. Missionaries supported the abolition of slavery. How was it that both the slave-owner and the abolitionist could proclaim the same religion?

The unity of humanity in Christ was evoked by the Christian theologian, but history indicates that in fact slavery and slave trading stopped only when they were no longer economical. It was the Industrial Revolution, not the gospel, that stopped slavery. The church itself had been heavily compromised. Toward the end of the fifteenth century, the Portuguese settled in the Congo, later in Angola. They received a mandate from their kings not only to trade but also to establish Christianity; they baptized the masses; they gave Portuguese titles to African rulers; they sent Africans overseas to be educated and trained for the priesthood. But in the midst of all this there was a strong alliance between the church and the institution of slavery. The Jesuit convent at São Paulo de Loanda was endowed with twelve thousand slaves, who were shipped to Brazil with the blessing of the bishop of Loanda (Westermann 1935, 125). In 1786, when William Carey proposed the settlement of slaves at Freetown at a Baptist meeting, the chairperson told him to sit down, saying only that the time was not ripe (CMS 1899, 81–100).

The Portuguese attempt to convert the people in West Africa (mostly Ghana) failed mainly because the people could not understand how the colonizers could preach love and enslave at the same time. Only minor signs of Christianity took hold. In Edina (Elmina), Gold Coast (now Ghana), the feast day of Saint Anthony was adopted into the local religious festivals. In the kingdom of Benin (Nigeria) the trappings of priestly dress were adopted by the royalty of the area. Evangelizing people about whom they knew little and cared nothing (except for their souls), the Portuguese could not possibly have "done theology" with them. All they left in Africa was superstition and the trappings of religion that have nothing to do with real life except perhaps to render mystifying what is not mysterious and so to push the genuine mysteries of life into the realm of magic.

SALVATION: COMMUNAL AND INDIVIDUAL

The "come apart and be saved" policy of the missionaries resulted in enclaves called "Christian villages." Because conversion meant not only a fitness of the individual for a future celestial life but also some attempt to make the world a more suitable place to which Christ should return, evangelical charity spilled into the world to touch the underprivileged. The emphasis however was on the individual—the context from which people came did not matter and was not seriously studied. The story of the missions is built on personalities, not on the transformation of communities. To effect a transformation of a whole community demanded more knowledge of the community than the missionaries could muster or their collaborators were willing to supply. So eventually the ten commandments became the yardstick for measuring sin so as to preach salvation. This legalistic approach to Christianity eventually crystallized into a religion of "thou shalt nots." Today among some Christian communities a "good" Christian is a person who is involved in a monogamous marriage and who does not smoke or drink or dance. The person may cheat a little and lie a little in public life, but certainly does not commit adultery.

Salvation for some individuals meant that they could not assume leadership roles in their traditional community. There was too much "heathenism" involved in being an African ruler, a position in which politics and religion coalesced, the sacred and the secular met. To be Christian, thou shalt not meddle with politics. The people of some African countries heard this kind of preaching during their struggles for independence. Involvement in the struggles was forbidden, especially if the activities were judged to be against the colonial powers.

The missionary told the Africans what they needed to be saved from, but when Africans needed power to deal with the spiritual realms that were real to them, the missionary was baffled. The ancestors were to be ignored; infant mortality and premature deaths were purely medical matters. Failure of rains and harvests were acts of God. Childlessness had nothing to do with witchcraft, nor was there any spiritual aspect to any other physical disorder or infirmity. The individual African in the process of being saved was told that witches do not exist, though the community continued to believe in the reality of evil that witchcraft represents. The missionaries' superficial assessment of the indigenous culture and its hold on the people who belong to it led to the Africans' superficial acceptance of Christianity.

WESTERNIZATION AND CHRISTIANIZATION

The theology of mission was, especially in the Roman Catholic enterprise, ecclesiocentric. All that obtained in the Latin countries of the West was to be duplicated in Africa. Western structures and Western standards of living were paid for by the West, so Africa, puzzled and awed, accepted them as necessary to the religion. But are they essential to Christianity? The close association of colonial power and particular denominations gave mission the appearance of an arm of colonialism.

The Holy Spirit transforms, making people quiet, devout, truthful, and industrious. The Spirit is a gift poured on all who believe in Christ. But then it seemed the age of the Spirit's work of leading into truth was over; only the established church had the truth.

The contradictions were many and complex, Jesus is our elder brother, the missionaries would preach. But the converts they made were not their twin brothers and sisters in Christ. The converts were younger and less capable; the missionaries had to think for them. After all, they, the missionaries, had been selected and sent by God. How were Africans to come to their own declaration of faith if they were required to follow blindly? How long did the missionary hope to remain the interpreter of Jesus to the "younger" siblings? Acceptance of the basic humanity of all human beings was only theoretical. In practice racism was central to the relationship between African and European. The chief reasons for this were ethnocentricity and greed. Separation of mission and church insured that black and white did not work together, let alone do the same type of job. Later this was to have implications for the financing of church development.

Needs were stimulated in light of the European lifestyle. They were not the needs of the people in Africa. Thus the structures created to meet these needs were European and Africans were ill at ease with them. Why the schools and the hospitals? These institutions were more in line with the work of salvation among Europeans than among Africans. But it seemed that being literate was one of the marks of being Christian. In terms of development, a government hospital or school could have achieved and often did achieve the same aims as the Christian hospital or school.

The spirit of sacrifice and dedication found among workers in the missionary institutions was unique, however, and it was this spirit that the African appreciated. The missionaries did not just preach sacrifice; they acted it out, and yet they lived apart, trying to live a European lifestyle in Africa. (We pitied them. They had not been properly "baked" and so could not survive hard life. So if they wanted to live apart, why not? Other ethnic groups did the same.) The dedication with which they ran their institutions was what set them apart as people who meant to be good neighbors.

The attempt to separate Christianity as a religion from Christianity as a way of life brought about a theological hiatus. The missionary movement was out to preach Liberty, Equality, and Fraternity in Christ, but not in matters political and cultural. This separation between material and spiritual salvation has been apparent throughout the modern missionary period and has operated both at home and abroad. Unhappy about the sociopolitical revolutions on the continent of Europe in the eighteenth and nineteenth centuries, the editor of *One Hundred Years: The Short History of the Church Missionary Society* wrote of the revolutionaries:

> They knew nothing of the *liberty* wherewith Christ makes his people free, nothing of the *equality* which rejoices that "the same Lord over all is rich unto all that call upon Him." Nothing of the *fraternity* involved in union with the elder brother under one Father [CMS 1899, 72].

He concluded that the CMS and not the protagonists of the French Revolution had the right to use the motto "Liberty, Equality, and Fraternity."

The liberty of the African converts was relative to this willingness to leave their African community. They were free to oppose their traditional rulers but not the missionary or the colonial government. They were the equal of the missionary and the white man before God, but for as long as they had to deal with the missionary they were minors, people of inferior "everything." They were children of God along with any other Christian, but as long as the missionary was with them the missionary was the elder, the one set apart, to be honored and obeyed. Although the missionaries were involved in charitable acts, they were not equipped ideologically to protest, let alone work against, incipient racism, exploitation, and other injustices. They accepted the structure of Western society as a given and did philanthropic work to alleviate the results of its injustices. A good deal of this benevolence was performed in the condescending manner we now call paternalism.

The contradiction here is that the missionaries did not accept the structure of African society. At every turn what they did worked toward its breakdown; they were veritable bulls in the African cultural china shop. Mbonu Ojike puts the blame on the "home training" the missionaries received. He described this training as bookish (theoretical), dogmatic, untried, ethnocentric, and lacking any appreciation for other cultures. He describes the products of this system who landed in Africa as falling into one of three types or categories. The first type was "sincere, respectable, somewhat bigoted but sufficiently devoted and self-sacrificing." These, he says, were very few. The second group was made up of "people who are disillusioned," and the third were "just job-seekers." But in the bags of all of them were packed absolute religious dogmas, Western legal thought, Western political ideas, Western social philosophy, Western economic theories, and an overall policy to compel the African to comply (Ojike 1955, 62).

The faithfulness of God in upholding the world in spite of all is a theme that runs through the African's own account of God. In 1819, a Christian convert in Sierra Leone who had witnessed the suffering, sickness, and eventual death of several missionaries wrote:

> I trust in the Lord Jesus: He knows his people,
> and He never left them, neither forsake them . . . .
> He knows what to do and I went to pray and I say
> "O Lord, take not all the teachers away from us"
> [CMS 1899, 41].

In 1836, the Fanti Methodists in Cape Coast carried on when all their missionaries died, one after the other. They said, "Though the missionary was dead, God lives" (Bartels 1965, 19; see *WMN* 1835, 8:367–368).

As is revealed in the above statement from Sierra Leone, African converts were willing to rely on Jesus and place great trust in him. Testimonies of conversion to Christianity provide interesting accounts of miraculous healings, dreams, visions, and salvation from evil influences. The spiritual power of the salvation story is what "bewitched" the African. It is therefore not strange that if relief from the evil influences, from the spiritual oppressors, is not felt by members of Christian churches, they move from church to church as well as to-and-fro between the church and the *Odunsini*, the traditional healer of body and soul. Nevertheless, Jesus, "the Great Physician," is the anchor of their faith, for he is preached as the healer par excellence (Hunter 1962; see also Sankey 1907). The cry for salvation/liberation in Africa is primarily a cry for health and wholeness.

3

Expressions, Sources, and Variants of African Theology

AFRICAN EXPRESSION AT THE SERVICE OF THEOLOGY

Oral Expression

"African theology" here describes the theological insights of African Christians. There are many if one cares to look for them. Long before the subject became fashionable, African Christians were trying to clarify and interpret for themselves the significance of salvation history, as well as stories about Jesus and stories told by him. Just as they had transmitted history orally, Africans retold these stories, elaborating them and drawing out what struck them as particularly relevant and enduring. This type of theology pervades the impromptu lyrics that Africans sang to interpret biblical events. There are several such songs heard from my paternal grandmother. Here is a lyric associated with the exodus:

The Compassionate God

Otwa-apem-esu na yɛ yen nam
Hɛn Egya ne yam ye o, Otwa apem esu a . . . yɛ nye no nam.
Ɔpatayinsuwa, Ɔdzebɔnkyɛ
Yɛ nye no nam.

We are walking with the one who caused a thousand to cross
   the waters.
Our Father is kind.[1]
The one who stops tears
The one who forgives sins.

All that God means to the congregation is expressed in these
songs. Other prayers they prayed echoed biblical events and spelled
out the faith of the people. Convinced that God hears the prayers
even of those in the belly of the whale, the people sang this lyric
based on the story of Jonah:

Out of the Deep

I am in the belly of the whale
in the depth of these waters
My God, when I call do hear me!

God who hears prayers from the deep
I am in the belly of the whale
Answer when I call!

My God my savior
My Lord and my God
Today I want to tell you something
Today I want to share my troubles
My Lord, answer when I call!

God is very near, close enough to hear when the African calls.
Many of these songs are still part of the African oral tradition,
but a few have been collected and stylized like those appended to
the *Christian Asor Ndwen*, the Fantse hymn book of Methodist
Church Ghana (Hunter 1972). *Ebibindwom* means literally "songs
of Africa."

Ebibindwom

Sunsum, soer yi Nyame ayew! . . .
Mo sunsum, soer yi N'ayew.
Sunsum, soer yi Ewuradze ayew! . . .
Mo sunsum, soer yi N'ayew.
N-hyira ɔnkà Nyankopɔn na Ne Ba!

N-daase ɔnkà Nyame Hen na Ne Ba!
N-tonton ɔnká Dɔfo Egya na Ne Ba!
Nyan, mo sunsum, soer yi N' ayew.

Spirit Arise

Spirit (alter ego) arise and praise God
Wake up my spirit, arise and praise him
Blessing be upon God and His Child[2]
Heap eulogies upon the gracious Father and His Child
Raise praises to God and His Child.

The content of the following song is similar to that of several psalms of the Hebrew Scriptures: All things praise God, wake up you human soul and do the same.

Osunsum e sɔr o
Beyi wo Nyame ayɛw o
ɔkra e sɔre o
Na wo Nyame fata ndaase o
Mmoadoma nyina sɔre
Woyi Nyame ayɛw o
Ntummoa so nyina sɔre
Woyi Nyame ayɛw o
Onyimpa ne kra e sɔre waka
beyi wo Nyame ayɛw o

Wake up soul, come and praise your God,
Wake up spirit for your God deserves thanks
All the animals wake up to praise God
All those who fly wake up to praise God
Human soul spring up and praise your God.

Other types of songs appear westernized and obviously evangelical, but even those are the songs of African Christians calling other Africans to the worship of God in Christ. One example:

Medze mo ho bɛma Nyame ne som pa
Dɛm ntsi mo nua dwen ho na bra.
Hɔn a wɔsɔm abosom wɔhwe ase
Hɔn a wɔsɔm Nyame n' w' ogyina pintsii.

I shall give myself to God's good worship (service)
Therefore my brother/sister think about this and come.
All those who worship the "divinities" fall down
Those who worship God stand firm.

In Nigeria the Christians adapted traditional themes, sentiments, and tunes to express their faith not just for themselves but as apologetics before their compatriots. Many of them had good reason not to become Christians or were Christians who felt the traditional rites could run *pari passu* with their newfound faith. Below is one such song sung by an aunt to my husband when he defiantly said he would not join in family ritual.

Ẹ jẹ k'a ṣ' orò ilé wa o
Ẹ jẹ k'a ṣ' orò ilé wa o
Ìgbàbó ò pé
Oníyé˙
Igbàgbó ò pé k'àwa ma ṣ'orò
Ẹ jé. k'a ṣ'orò ilé wa o.

Let us practice the rituals of our family,
Let us practice the rituals of our family.
     The Christian faith does not say
     The Christian faith does not say we shouldn't.
Let us practice the rituals of our family.

The aunt too was a Christian. In answer to such a reminder of the demands of the religious milieu, this lyric was composed and sung to the same tune:

Ẹ t'Ọlórun l'àwa óò ṣeo
Ẹ t'Olúwa l'àwa óò ṣe o
Èṣù ń ṣe ṣá
Óníyé
Èṣù nṣe ṣá kò lè rí bi gbà
É t'Olúwa l'awa óò ṣe o

Ah! It is God's will we will do.
Ah! It is God's will we will do.

The Devil is trying I say
The Devil is trying but can't find a way.
Ah! It is God's will we will do.

This next lyric comes from South Africa. It was composed by "a native convert together with the tune . . ." and was sung "by the natives with great feeling. Very often the singing is interrupted by loud outbursts of feeling, especially by old Christians" (*WMN* 1857, 3:7-9).

Thou art the Great God: he who is in heaven
It is Thou, thou Shield of Truth
It is Thou, thou Tower of Truth
It is Thou, thou Bush of Truth
It is Thou, thou who sittest in the highest.

Thou art the Creator of Life
Thou madest the regions above
The Creator who made the heavens also
The maker of the stars and the Pleiades

The shooting stars declare it unto us.
The maker of the blind, of thine own will
Didst thou make them.
The Trumpet speaks, for us it calls.

Thou art the Hunter who hunts for souls
Thou art the Leader who goes before us
Thou art the Great Mantle which covers us
Thou art He whose hands are with wounds
Thou art He whose feet are with wound
Thou art He whose blood is a trickling stream
Thou art He whose blood was spilled for us.

And why?
For this great price we call
For thine own place we call.

Here we find primitive Christianity with a binitarian statement that could have come from a pre-Nicean theologian. God is truth; God is great; and the crucified Christ brings us salvation. These affirmations are at the core of black theology in South Africa, where "sense and nonsense about God" are being actively explored.[3]

This oral theology has not to my knowledge been systematically collected in Africa. Collecting them is an important task for us to undertake if we are really to appreciate the religion of those who sing these songs. Oral theology is used in Sunday school lessons and in preaching (H. W. Turner 1965; Oosthuizen 1979, 2). To distill the theology that inspires and informs those oral expressions will be to put one's finger on part of the theology of the people in the pews.

Theological expression may also be found in sculpture and in drama (Cupitt 1977, 133-147; Sofola 1979, 83-94). Those researching the symbolism of Africa's primal religions find meanings for colors and numbers (Mveng 1979, 83-94). Victory in my culture, for example, is marked by white. If you see people with white clay (*hyirew*) marks on their bodies, you know that they have been successful in one of life's battles, be it childbirth or a case in court. Red (*ntwoma*-Laterite) markings spell gloom, disaster, and even despair. The choice of white clothes by Methodist Church Ghana for communion service and Easter and New Year celebrations is not fortuitous. White clothing is the raiment of a people who trust in the victorious God. The white worn by several of the Aladura churches may also indicate this as well as the concept of purity while it serves further to promote egalitarianism. Certainly the symbols in the liturgies are bound to give more meaning to worship. Candles, holy water, the removal of sandals, and the exclusion of menstruating women from inside the church all have theological implications, most of which pertain to primal religious views that are reinforced by Hebrew religion as presented in the Hebrew Scriptures.

Written Expression

The body of African written theology grows with increased publication of theses, books, and journals specifically on theology. The people also see Christian theology in the novels and plays written by Africans. Other written sources of theology include reports of church meetings both denominational/ecumenical and local/

international/continental. A substantial bibliography is accumulating (Mbiti 1979).

SOURCES

The Bible

All Africans who theologize do so from some common roots or sources. First of course is the Bible. Even for those who cannot read, the Bible is a living book. If they cannot read, they have it read to them. It is something of a marvel to listen to Obadare, the blind evangelist of the Christ Apostolic Church in Nigeria. He calls for a passage to be read, repeats it with the reader, and then comments on it.

Africans identify with much in the Bible, and therefore much in the Bible remains in their memory and becomes the basis for their reflections about God. Christianity lives on in the constant telling and retelling of the story of the Christ-event; Christian theology comes out of these events and narratives with which the people identify. Whether read in a village or studied in a university, the Bible is accepted as the source for the articulation of the Christian faith.

In English-using Africa, a course called Bible Knowledge is taught throughout the primary school. A similar course is continued through the secondary level until the student chooses not to take the exit exam in that subject. At the exit exam stage, African Traditional Religion is added. At the tertiary level, religious studies become a matter of specialization and the approaches and emphases vary. Those who take part in particular Christian studies programs are expected to undertake studies in the history and religion of Israel, the history and foundations of the Christian faith, and biblical languages for the purposes of translation and exegesis. All this amounts to a good deal of exposure to Christian teaching.

Christian History and African History

African Christian theology is also rooted in history. Jesus of Nazareth was a man who walked this earth. Christian faith becomes fully relevant only as it is allowed to be informed by the history of Christianity both at the level of dogmatic development and its application to life which is sometimes called pastoral theology. The traditional themes of God, creation, sin, and redemption are emphasized in African theology. The central theme to my mind is the reign of God. John the Baptist announced it, and Jesus gave it priority in his preaching and continually demonstrated its style and power.

Part of the church's historical reality with which African theology deals is Africa's own history—its social institutions as well as its religious and cultural values in all their variety. These historical realities include our dependent economies, the exploitation of the rural and the voiceless, the power of the family and of rites, the political experiments geared to forging a system that answers to Africa's vision of a just society and contributes to the world community of the twentieth century. The experience of conquest, the appropriation of authority by non-natives, of slavery and of co-option are all valid sources of African theology because they are an integral part of the African experience.

VARIANTS

Theology, to be authentic and relevant, must reflect a particular context. At the same time, if the theology is Christian it cannot help but throw light upon some universal issue. A monolithic construction of African theology would be unrealistic, given the variety in the continent of historical experience, political systems (traditional and colonial), primal religion, and economies. In Africa there exist at least three broad theological trends: the traditional, the indigenized, and the contextual.

Traditional Theology

Some traditional African theologians are convinced that all the theology needed to fix Christianity firmly into Africa has already been done. If the proclamation of the Christ-event and the telling of Bible stories was good enough for my grandmother then it should be good enough for me. Anything beyond this is suspect.

Another traditional opinion holds that the systematic theology taught in European (and therefore African) seminaries is sufficient and one does not need to ask whether or not this theology makes sense to Africans today. Most sermons on the person of Christ simply state as a matter of fact that Jesus is God and Man. All that is required of the African is assent. On Trinity Sunday preachers throw up their hands: the Trinity is a mystery and part of our faith; if you do not accept it then you are not Christian.

For both types of traditional theologians, the Bible is the only valid source of Christian theology. It may be supplemented by the traditional creeds, but nothing more is allowed or needed.

Indigenized Theology

The indigenizers begin from the position of the traditionalists, but they go on to ask how far the Hebrew worldview and the Greco-Roman symbols that permeate the Bible and Christianity are understood by African Christians. The preoccupation is that if they are not really understood, the religion will not be well rooted. Some Africans (including myself) have sought the help of the symbols and language of the primal religions of Africa, knowing full well that their use has limited value and may even be misconstrued as a call for the return to primal religious beliefs and practices. Merely using these symbols does not get at the heart of the problem for a number of reasons. The symbols of the primal religions come to some African Christians second-hand: they read about them in books; they watch festivals and rituals without understanding their meaning; they have become spectators, alien to their own environment. The use of these symbols implies that if the African really understood the doctrines as taught by the missionaries, Christianity would have been more rooted in the culture. The symbols provide only a partial view of the historical context of the church. Their use assumes that there is an essence of the Christian faith that may be distilled from the trappings of cultures that had accepted it before it reached Africa. This view (espoused by Charles Nyamiti and Vatican II) is applauded until one comes to draw the lines.

It is generally accepted that in order

> that African theology should evolve one has first to find out in the sources of revelation the essential and universal Christian values and adapt them afterwards to the African mentality and needs. This seems almost self-evident [Nyamiti 1969, 3].

Some criticized this trend because it could breed syncretism.[4] For such people syncretism is of course always negative. Some Africanist scholars see the whole exercise as the coopting of primal religion to the support of Christianity, which they believe by itself will not survive in Africa (p'Bitek 1970, chaps. 6 and 7). Others say it demotes primal religion to the position of a *praeparatio evangelica*. They maintain it should not be in this position because it is by and in itself an adequate response to Africa's religious experience (see Idowu 1973, chap. 6). My position is that the Christian theologian would be unrealistic to ignore the point at which religion is the deepest element in Africa's living culture. Time given to the study of rites of initiation and reconciliation in African societies, of the relationship of persons to communities is time well spent. The identity crisis in Africa, especially among the urbanized, the Western-educated, and the Christians, may be attributed to the loss of a dynamic perspective on life, which comes from knowing and living one's religio-cultural history. We cannot expect those who cannot tell their story, who do not know where they come from, to hear God's call to his future.[5] We cannot expect a people "without a history" to respond as responsible human beings living in Africa. If their story is the same as the story of those who live in Europe and America, then they can only echo Euro-American responses. To indigenize traditional theology, limited as it is, is still more relevant than to open Euro-American theological cans.

Contextual Theology

The third variant might be called contextual theology. It is not that the indigenization theologians are not contextual, but that their contextualization is often limited to socioreligious elements of African life. Contextualization here expands to include the politico-economic aspects of life and seeks to produce symbols and language that are universal and inclusive of Africa's reality. We might call this a political theology. It is a theology that aims to confront society with the Bible and intends to read the Bible from the perspective of the people.

Here the basic controversy is over the question "who are the people?" In relation to Africa this is not a theoretical question. Africa's people are those who have known what it means to be conquered: they are servants not masters, they belong to the poor not to the rich world, they form part of those who have no voice, not of those who have the dominant voice. They are black not white. It is from this position that the Bible is read. Without standing where they stand you cannot hear what they hear. Black theology from South Africa is the African example of liberative theology (Boesak 1972).

Much of this theology is of course different from traditional dogmatics and from the clusters of theological themes that are offered as well-reasoned systems of thought by Africa's Western and Western-oriented theology teachers. While they struggle to explain the omnipotence, omniscience, and supreme authority of God, contextual theologians seek relational symbols to narrate human dependence upon God (Ntwana 1973).

The contextual theologians are attempting to stand where they can hear and to let the voice from the Bible challenge how they and others live and how they can give expression to their faith in the living God through the faith and hope that is in Christ.

4

Conventional Dogmatics on African Soil

AFRICA'S PRIMAL RELIGIONS

The prevailing issue in mission-oriented theology is that of idolatry. The Christian message to Africa is simple: there is only one God, and God is to be reached and worshipped only through Jesus Christ; any other way, however noble, moral, and ethical, is idolatrous. Around this central theme the religious implications and the content of African sociopolitical practices fall into place for discussion. Are the nature divinities rivals to God (the Source Being) or are they God's agents or messengers (angels)? Should African Christians become rulers of their people? Would they compromise their Christianity by taking part in traditional festivals as chief priests and representatives of their peoples? The ancestors, the part of the family that lives in the unseen world—are they worshipped, are they intermediaries, or are they called upon to join the living in praying to God who alone orders all things? *Sę Onyame nkum wo a ǫdasani ntumi nyę hwee,* "If God has not killed you, no human being can harm you." Traditional oaths and covenants—do they conflict with the Christian covenant symbolized by baptism into Christ and into his resurrection and death, with the redemption that Christ alone brings from sin, death, and all that oppresses our humanity? Does belonging to a traditional cult conflict with a Christian's membership in the community of the redeemed in the church? The Spirit that operates in the primal religion of Africa—is it the same Spirit of God through which God gives us grace to do good works and to have faith? The "trials" that happen after death in the "court of the ancestors"—how do they relate to God's judgment in this life and in the hereafter? The "life-plan" (*Nkrabea*) that we acquire before coming into this world and the soul (*Okra*) that carries it—do they have anything to do with what the theologian of Genesis 1 calls "the image of God" in us.

Circumcision (male or female); polygyny, female-husbands, or other types of "marriages"; initiation into adulthood; facial scarring have become red herrings used to postpone the hard theological debate on Christianity and culture; and are used as polemics in the attempt to Westernize and to Christianize in one go. In the churches they have been matters of discipline not of theology. I think these themes have occupied far more space than they are worth. Seldom is there an attempt to delineate the theological and ethical issues involved.

Scholars, both black and white, who were seriously concerned to find out what the African believes, laid the groundwork for African Christian theology by studying African traditional religion. I refer to traditional religion in these essays as the primal religion of Africa because it is the religion of Africa unadulterated by Islam, Christianity, or any other system of belief.[1] I do not call it "traditional" because that word implies something "customary," something practiced without modification, or unthinkingly carried on just because that is how it has always been. "Traditional" can imply a religion that is dying, being replaced by the new with which it is fruitlessly competing, a conservative and conserving religion bearing little relationship to the times.

The writings of Parrinder, Idowu, and Mbiti are examples of the systematic effort to understand the primal religion of Africa (see Parrinder 1961; Idowu 1965a; Mbiti 1975). More detailed research is available in African universities. Researchers so far have come from the Christian church. The scholars tend to sound unconvincing in their conclusions; they seem to be writing to illumine the West rather than to produce in depth information on the primal religion of Africa for Africans. Several papers have criticized their efforts because these Christian scholars stop short of confessing that we Africans do not really need Christianity or Islam to tell us of God and of our total dependence on divine providence and guidance. The scholars seem to struggle at the end of their theses to explain why Christianity is still needed. Okot p'Bitek, of the University of Nairobi, represents this criticism (p'Bitek 1970, 107–111).

Just how difficult it is to produce a convincing apologia for Christianity was evidenced at each end-of-year interview we had at the Religious Studies Department of the University of Ibadan. The question put was: "If African traditional religion is as you have found it, are you going to continue to convert people from it?" The answer was almost always Yes, and the reason given was usually that the Bible says Jesus is the only Way. Most students fumble through questions relating to the particularity of Jesus Christ and what that has to do with "becoming Christian" (a member of a church). This shows no lack of maturity or sophistication; it is an issue that the whole of the people of Christ struggle with in one connection or another. As for the academic study of the primal religion, the way forward may be found in reading the detailed research being published (minus the conclusions) as well as the even more crucial literature coming from those who adhere to the primal religions, for example, Dr. Wande Abimbola's collection of the Ifa Corpus of Divination (Abimbola 1975).

A REORIENTATION OF PRIMAL RELIGIONS

C. G. Baëta of Ghana, in a series of lectures on liberation theology (April 1981), astonished his audience with his apologia for Christianity. In his first lecture he reviewed the intellectual contribution of the late J. B. Danquah, in whose honor the lectures were given. Baëta said that Danquah's exposition on God in Akan religion is so profound that those who read him are bound to say the Akan do not need Christianity to tell them about God or to teach them how to live "the good life."

All applauded, and they were not all Akan. (Accra, where the lecture was given, is Ghana's capital and a university city.) In his third and final lecture, which was devoted to the subject of African theology, Baëta questioned the location of research and teaching of African traditional religion in African universities. Does this research not belong in African studies rather than in departments set up to specialize in religion? He went on to question the validity of using concepts, beliefs, and practices from the primal religion as "building blocks" for Christian theology in Africa. He queried whether we have now or shall ever have the full picture of what African primal religion is. He asked: What is its value for the constructing of theology and theory? Do we not need an African philosophy relative to dogmatics in the way the early church related to neo-Platonism, medieval European Christianity to Aristotelianism, and contemporary Christianity to various currents of modern European and American philosophies? When we have answered all these questions, he said, "then we shall still be left with the need for developing a hermeneutic for its [the primal religion] interpretation and application" (Baëta 1981).

These are questions that several African theologians ask. Baëta went on to a startling statement. He said that every nation can show the indigenous traits that are suitable for Christian use, that God chose the Jewish people as his instrument for the instruction of the rest of the world in order that all people might be saved. The structured view of the world's creation, redemption, and consummation, he said, is complete in Christianity. It is a datum, a given. Local materials may be used to clarify knotty points but they cannot be considered new building materials. Can the ideas of African religion provide a better foundation than the Hebrew Scriptures for Christian theology? This, he said, should not be the objective of Christians studying African theology.[2]

For African theologians like Baëta, the theology the West has given us is sufficient and can be absorbed into the bloodstream of African Christianity. We need not look for new ingredients, just new recipes from the old ingredients. Baëta thinks that African theologians should be taking the received theology and reviewing it in the face of the needs of modern Africa, socioeconomic and political but not the religiocultural.

I understand Baëta to say that the received Christian dogmatics is sufficient to build a theology that is both meaningful and liberating. If one follows the liberation theology of Latin America one would have to agree. Baëta may be understood as saying that we in Africa have to read the Bible from the perspective of the poor and the marginalized, those who have known foreign rule with all its consequences. This may include giving the books of the Maccabees their proper place in the Protestant Bible together with Moses,

Amos, Isaiah, and Joel. We may have to look squarely at the power and the will of God and study afresh the Hebrew idea of the consummation of history and the end of this world in a linear way. We may have to give these ideas their proper place as we retell history from the underside and see God at work in *our* history too. I believe that a universal does not make much sense apart from its particulars. So any selection from the so-called universal Christian dogmas in Africa should be what responds to Africa's needs.

Baëta contends that much has been left unattended to even in the commands of Christ—not that we do not know them or that they go against our culture but simply that as human beings we continue to pay lip service to the good we know. He says:

> There are so many poor, so many disadvantaged, so many marginalized struggling for the realization of the most primitive, most elemental qualities of human living. . . . Yet others have surpluses both in Africa and in the northern countries [Baëta 1981].

For Baëta to be a theologian in Africa is to join in the church's mission, which he says is "here and now to be the sign of Christ's presence in the liberation of our community from unrighteousness of all kinds and from oppressive structures" (Baëta 1981). "Christ," he says, "came to set men free from their own selfishness." This, he claims, is the business of theology, to effect in humanity what will make for its liberation from sin and to strengthen (*stērizō*) the other disciples (Lk 22:32).

I can only applaud Baëta's thesis concerning the central business of African theology. I do not know how one could go about this business while totally ignoring Africa's whole culture including its religion. The hold of culture is such that it cannot be set aside. I do not believe that the African experience can be completely replaced by the Jewish one if we are trying to understand how God has always been and how God continues to be active in Africa's history. Karl Barth was prepared to discountenance the so-called general revelation and so to ignore a basic principle of education to progress from the known to the unknown. The Bible is the cornerstone of African theology, but I would not understand the oppressiveness of eighth–century (B.C.) Israel and the reality lived by its suffering masses without the experience of the trade pattern in Ghana and Africa as a whole. It was Baëta who likened the market women of West Africa to the Kine of Bashan (Baëta 1960). The women may be the immediate symbols of the fetters of injustice; behind them is the cotton industry of Manchester and the cotton pickers around the world.

The Bible is the cornerstone of African theology and of all Christian theology for that matter. But a cornerstone is not the whole edifice. The hermeneutical circle necessary for the understanding of the Bible and theology cannot be bypassed.

REJECTION OF PRIMAL RELIGIONS

Another type of today's African dogmaticians might quarrel with Baëta's plea to make Christian ideals more operative in the daily lives of Africans so that the ideals might minister to sociopolitical and economic needs. Byang Kato sees this as placing undue emphasis on horizontalism, which seeks well-being here and now to the neglect of eternal heaven and hell. This "distorted view of salvation" is the outcome of universalism, which Baëta decries (Kato 1975, 144-145, 158). The preoccupation with well-being, Kato claims, is the domain of the primal religions and is to be rejected, because "what will it profit a man, if he gains the whole world and forfeits his life?" (Mt 16-26).

For Kato the only reason to study Africa's primal religions is to expose the idolatry that they are and to reduce their hold on the culture of the people. In his *Theological Pitfalls*, Kato exhibits his abhorrence of heresy, in this case the universalism, which he sees being promoted by the universities that study African Traditional Religion, Islam, and Christianity in one department. E. B. Idowu and John Mbiti and all that they stand for are at the receiving end of these attacks. So too is the ecumenical movement in Africa, symbolized for Kato by the All Africa Conference of Churches (AACC). The generation of theologians that knew Kato personally hesitate to respond to the assertions in his book now that he is dead (Mbiti 1979, 85). Kato's successor as secretary to the Evangelical Association of Africa and Madagascar, Adeyemo Tokunbo (also of Dallas Theological Seminary), has published a kind of sequel to *Theological Pitfalls* called *Salvation in African Traditional Reli-*

gion and has researched "the persistence and continuity of Yoruba piety and religion in Ibadan" (Adeyamo 1979, chaps. 1 and 2). Adeyemo continues the Kato tradition and follows his suggestion that we need more in-depth study of the primal religions. Kato himself set the example in *Theological Pitfalls* by studying his own people, the Hahm, whom he prefers to call the Jaba, the name given them by their Hausa colonizers (Kato 1975, 27). In his presentation of Hahm religion he "condemns and dismisses the so-called heathenism of Africa" (Grau 1968, 66), enthusiastically following the standard Western Christian attitude toward the primal worldview of African beliefs and practices.

This rejection [of the] African worldview by an African shows how successful the Christian missions were in alienating Africans from their "Africanness." Objectivity is one thing, but going to Africa's primal religious beliefs and practices with the intention of demonstrating how far they fall short of the Euro-American Christian ideal is another. Kato pleads that "the true gospel that has transformed the lives of some fifty percent [of the] Jaba people must not be adulterated"; he believes that the traditional religion, which he tells us sees the Supreme Being, Nom, as "the greater than which we cannot conceive," should be totally set aside (Kato 1975, 29).

PRIMACY OF THE BIBLE

Christian dogmatics are to be taught only from the Bible and should above all focus on the salvation of the soul. In the criticisms Kato levelled against others and in his positive statements I identify four theological insights. They follow the insights of the missionary theology described above and are in fact embedded in traditional Christian dogmatics. They are:

1. Those outside Christ are perishing; if they do not hear the gospel they will be lost forever.

2. Theology should place less emphasis on the "horizontal" and more on the "vertical."

3. Accepting Christ here and now settles the question of where you will spend eternity. In light of this, doctrines relating to heaven and hell should be prominent.

4. Salvation is the monopoly of Christianity, and its parameters are to be found in the Bible alone (Kato 1975, 141, 67, 174).

These four principles should be the foundations for Christian theology in Africa for "the soul-salvation concerned believer" (Kato 1975, 178-179). Phrases such as "accepting Christ" and "eternal redemption from sin" need to be clarified and concretized if theology is to be more than appending one's signature to a series of propositions.

The authority of the Bible is another element of dogma now being highlighted. The plea is not only for the centrality of the Bible in Christian theology but also, as Kato puts it, "the inerrancy of the Bible in the original manuscripts and faithfully translated" (Kato 1975, 182). The question of "original manuscripts" is itself a highly specialized study. In addition, many Africans who do theology, both scholarly and popular, do not operate comfortably in Greek, Hebrew, and Aramaic and most in none of these languages. Few have so much as seen an "original" manuscript. A positive step is the current effort being made to replace the African-language Bibles originally translated from the King James version with direct translations from original languages by African scholars under the auspices of the United Bible Societies.

The crucial question lies in the meaning of "inerrancy," which is beginning to die the death of a thousand qualifications. This is an area of study that needs the application of more African theological resources. This might enable us to escape the Euro-American perspective from which we now view Scripture. Perhaps entirely new questions need to be raised concerning the Bible. What is the intrinsic value in telling and retelling these stories? Those of us involved in this area of endeavor look forward to the publication of translations and commentaries of the Bible by Africans who know the original languages. Meanwhile biblical stories are told, and many people are converted or comforted. They look to the salvation of their souls and a place in heaven when they leave this body behind. The content of such a faith remains a necessary question.

Kato, "a Bible-believing Christian," does not actually treat the various themes of Christian theology—this was not his aim. His stated aim was to point out the theological pitfalls that "only a discerning spirit-filled Bible-believer can see and refute." His book is basically a refutation of what he calls "liberal ecumenism," "universalism," an African theology that he sees as a watering down or a compromise of the gospel in order to impress the world with an African contribution (Kato 1975, 176). This effort he considers childish. If African theology is only done to impress the world, then one might indeed call it childish. However, I do not see impressing the world as the aim. Who is the South African trying to impress if she retells the exodus story to underline the insight that God is on the side of the oppressed? The courage to be can best be inspired in South Africa by South African theologians and only if Christians can hear and believe it will affect them as it should.

The idea of primal religions as *praeparatio evangelica* is the outcome of the christocentric character of Christianity, but the claim that Christianity is the only line of communication between human beings and God is debatable. Revelation too has become a focus of African theology. This followed the recognition that primal religious views are similar to those found in the Bible. Kato concludes from his inquiry into his people's religion that "apart from the general revelation and the fact of the vestiges of Imago Dei, direct revelation of God to leaders of other religions is highly improbable." This conclusion comes from the answer Kato's informer, Gin Maigari, gives to his question: "Has God spoken directly with the religious leaders?" Maigari said: "I know that my people have some knowledge of Nom. But as to where they got it, I do not know. I don't think Nom spoke to our leaders face to face as he is so remote."

What do we mean by "God speaks"? How do we "see God face to face"? In questioning people about their religious experience we should not limit the terms of the experience to the biblical narratives, for God must be allowed to communicate with people on the wavelength most appropriate to them. God alone can know that wavelength. Kato, however, had decided the answer before the question, because for him "it is most unlikely that either Jaba or any other non-Christian peoples have received a direct revelation from God." At this stage, I do not know where he places the Hebrew scriptures.

Faith in God, to whom all history belongs, demands the belief that with the coming of Christ and the promise of the Holy Spirit all who acknowledge the sovereignty of God are let into all truth. If honest efforts to situate theology in Africa produce "unhealthy trends which are a cause for alarm, a tendency towards a dilution of truth, mixture of nationalism and continued tribalism, a confusion over the meaning of Salvation,"[3] the effort should still be made in the service of the mission of the church; the owner of the church will purify and use it. For it is an effort to be open to what God is saying to the churches and to the world.

Whatever African theology becomes and whatever its association with Africa's primal religions, Christian theology is not what Kato claims. The primal religions do not need Christian scholars in order to survive. Kato's observation that "the defunct gods of African traditional religion are rearing their heads" (Kato 1975, 173) has nothing to do with theologians. The gods were never defunct. A Christian-oriented Western culture tried to suppress them, but they never died.

If Christian theology is convincing, the gods may become unnecessary and their worship and feast days merge into sociocultural events that have no spiritual hold on a majority of people. The Christian theology that displaced the gods of the primal religions of Europe did not do so by simply declaring that those gods were dead and their feast days of no effect. Instead several concepts and celebrations passed imperceptibly into Christian theology. The use of the four Lenten candles in many churches, symbolizing the association of Jesus Christ with light, shows how a positive view of pre-Christian religious concepts from whatever source may be the vehicle through which God is revealed. I believe that an African theology devoid of African primal worldviews would be poor indeed. Our redemption in Christ should lead us to live freely as children of God who have encountered God's will in their situation.

In the early 1970s the World Mission and Evangelism Division of the World Council of Churches promoted a study, "Salvation Today," which led to a critical examination of the theology of salvation and a debate as to whether "salvation" carried the same connotation as the word "liberation." The Kato School, or rather the African wing of conservative evangelical theology, was very active in the debate. We shall return to this theme. I consider it to be one of the cardinal themes in Christian theology in Africa today, and one on which a great divide might develop if we do not give it adequate attention.

Today we have entered an era of polemics in which some Christians are described as Bible-believing, Spirit-filled, soul-salvation seekers, with the implication that others are not. To the onlooker who is not of the Christian community, the criteria for being "Christian" would be taken from the saying of Jesus Christ that by their fruits they shall be known (Mt. 7:16). What is the theology in which saying and doing will coincide? To work diligently toward this type of theology is, in my view, the task of the Christian theologian today. Whether in Africa or elsewhere, the motivation of theology should be the search for the modus vivendi that demonstrates our covenant relationship with God.

5

Theology from a Cultural Outlook

Few today would dispute the statement that theology is a field not unaffected by history and culture. Even the myths by which we express religious intuitions that are beyond words and beyond history are constructed out of experience. Our human yearning to fathom the unknown, life, the differentiation of existence, death, and that which is beyond death is at the base of the creation stories that are found in primal worldviews including that of the Hebrews. Similarly, our hope that chaos will give place to order, isolation to communion, and death to life is also born of experience.

At the center of the Hebrew story is a God of compassion who suffers with the world to keep it from falling apart. A feeling of dependence on an Order-Of-Things and Beings beyond us and on an Ever-Ordering-Being or Vital Force which led Abraham to walk away from the delta that was gradually getting overpopulated. He later became known as the man who walked with God.[1] We human beings do feel a part of, as well as a dependence upon, a greater structure of reality that transcends what we can comprehend. When Moses began his rationalization of Hebrew religion, it was within the experience of what oppression in the land of plenty could do to a people.[2] The theology of separation of powers attributed to Jesus has to be read in the context of an oft-colonized people who professed a religion of total dependence upon God.[3] When Paul exhorted the Christian women of Corinth to curb the enthusiasm issuing from their new-found freedom, it was to ensure that Christians do nothing that might stand in the way of their primary aim of making Christ known in all the world. His use of the myths of creation was culturally determined; so also were the injunctions he drew from the pool of Jewish theological thinking.

Missionary theology burst upon Africa south of the Sahara after the Protestant Reformation by way of pietists and evangelicals, whose nations were experiencing the power of steam and gunpowder. This theology clashed with African culture, which was pious in its own right but had no steam engines and rifles and was by no stretch of imagination evangelical in the sense of going out to tell its own good news to other nations. The missionaries reflected their culture in the symbols they brought along and in their telling of the story of salvation.

Nonetheless, Christians in the West were surprised when African Christianity began to wear African clothes. The exclusive leadership of the West in a religion that professed to liberate Africans from the power of their natural rulers and priests and from the demands of their primal religions was questioned. The Aladura churches[4] have today become objects of study. Western churches, Anglicans, Methodists and Presbyterians in Africa energetically join to study this African Christian phenomenon. Would that the same spotlight were being thrown on *their* adopted denominational theologies, church practices, vestments, discipline, preaching, and rites, and that these would all be subjected to the touchstone of the religion of Jesus of Nazareth.

Debates surrounding the cultural aspects of African theology take place not only among missionaries, theologians, and historians of religion and sociologists, not only among Western Christians, but also in Africa and among Africans, and have become a central preoccupation of Christians of all types. Among Roman Catholics the whole issue has brought back onto scholarly pages and around conference tables discussions of the efforts of Matteo Ricci and Roberto de Nobili, who faced the strong cultures of China and India in the sixteenth and seventeenth centuries (Latourette 1955, 931–933, 939–941; Motte and Lang 1982).

One clear line of thinking holds that African culture has to be transformed by Christ, and that what we should look at is the *inculturation process*. To speak of acculturation is to suggest that

Christ should become "domesticated" in Africa. At the center of this debate is the meaning we give to *Skēncō* (see Jn 1:14), "tabernacled," to be "at home" among human beings without dampening the divine glory. How should we understand the manner of Jesus living among us? It is interesting to note that the alternative word *Katoikeō*, which contains the word *house*, was not used, but rather the word for a *movable tent*. Some of us involved in this search find that we have to look again at all that we have been taught by our parents, pastors, and professors concerning the incarnation and its meaning in Christianity. The unique theological factor that Christianity introduced into Africa was the incarnation. We shall have to see how the doctrine of the incarnation functions or should function in African theology.

We turn now to some of the attempts at inculturation/ acculturation of Christianity in black Africa. Acculturation will be used to refer to the efforts of Africans to use things African in their practice of Christianity, inculturation as the manifestation of changes that have come into the African way of life as a result of the Christian faith. I am well aware that both descriptions are deficient, but this is not the place for that debate. These terms will be clarified in the process of doing theology in Africa. We cannot pause for courses in African philosophy before we express what we believe as Christians in Africa. The formal and systematic study of African philosophy being done in our universities will of course interact with the Christian theological task as it unfolds in Africa and may in the end render our "–culturation" language of no substance.

ACCULTURATION

I first became aware of a new horizon in my own formation as an African Christian when I moved out of the Methodist schools I had been attending into Achimota school. Looking back, I now realize that there was a deliberate effort to keep the products of the Achimota school from becoming alienated from their natural milieu while they were receiving an "English education" in a boarding school staffed by black and white teachers. Among these teachers was Owura Ephraim Amu, who taught music. He alone of all the teachers had a title in a Ghanaian language; this made him the jumping-off place for endless student debates on the meaning of being African. All the male teachers were called "Mister"; he alone was called *Owura*, "Master," in Akan. He was a living legend. He never wore a European suit, but always a pair of shorts and a short-sleeved, collarless shirt made of hand-woven, undyed local cotton to all everyday informal gatherings, classes, and church services. On formal occasions, he added Ntama, the "Great-Cloth" (a Roman-type Ghanaian toga).

He taught us Western music, piano, violin, and oboe. We sat motionless, listening for the ripples of water in Handel's *Water Music*. We read the biographies of J. S. Bach, Beethoven, Tchaikovsky. But Amu was at his most impressive when he taught us how to produce Ghanaian rhythms on drums, rattles, and gongs and how to dance to each rhythm. He convinced the students who were already advanced in these skills before coming to Achimota to work at passing the traditions on.

He taught us "Nymphs and Shepherds fly away" and "Hiawatha's Wedding" and some French songs too. But what we talked about in our many sessions on this "strange" man were his own compositions in Twi and Ewe. Here are some examples:

"Yen ara Asase ni": This land is ours. (We cannot allow claims to superior knowledge, crooked dealings, and selfishness to ruin this land which the ancestors acquired and retained for us with their blood.)
"Adawura bọ me": Ring on, gong! (A delightful round that teaches the sounds to two musical instruments.)
"Okofo Kwasi barima": Kwasi, the warrior man. (Go back and pick it up. You have left it behind—knowledge, peace, wealth. . . .)

Those of us who sang in the choir and gave the school an atmosphere for Christmas, Good Friday, and Easter had additional tales to tell. Amu's dictum was that all is voluntary until you have opted for it; then it becomes compulsory. He required diligence, seriousness, and faithfulness of his groups of budding musicians and singers. Even today I find myself singing those songs when the seasons come round. Here is my Good Friday favorite:

Ewurade no nim na ǫbɛhwɛ ara
Onim Okunafo n'ahia sɛm
na ǫrennyaw no ho ara da ǫbehwɛ
ǫbaa hwɛ wo ba ni
Na wo aberante hwɛ wo na ni
Ewurade no nim na Ǫbɛhwɛ ara.

"The Lord who in times past cared for the widow and the orphan will look upon you." This song is based on the words of Jesus from the cross to the beloved disciple and to his mother (Jn 19:26–27). God's compassion, the enduring theme of popular theology, is reechoed here.

Owura Amu, an educated African Christian, said to my generation that God was in our midst before the white man came. Another level of the acculturation debate in my experience also revolved around Amu. An incident in his life has become a classic example of the lack of sensitivity to African culture on the part of the early carriers of the Christian message.

Owura Amu was once refused the pulpit of the Presbyterians (then Basel Mission) because he went to his appointment wearing the Ghanaian toga. I hasten to add that this contempt for African traditional clothing, even when modified by European fashions, was found not only in the church but also among the anglicized Ghanaians, especially those on the coast. My mother remembers a lawyer who, seeing his daughter wearing African traditional dress, exploded: "Off you go and get dressed. I thought you were one of these *adesefo* [villagers] who come here to sell *dǫkon* [a wrapped dumpling of corn dough]."

The African clergy has only recently attempted to adapt African clothing into the liturgical garments of the clergy. After Vatican II African colors and patterns appeared in the stoles of Catholic priests in Nigeria. Rev. Margaret Boamah-Secu hallowed the clothes the Ghanaian lawyer ridiculed by wearing a Roman shirt and collar with an African skirt to celebrate Holy Communion in Ibadan at the closing worship of the consultation of African women theologians. (September 1980).

On the whole, however, it is the Roman Catholic church, not the Euro-American Protestant churches in Africa, which has taken acculturation seriously. Drums have ceased to be symbols of paganism (in the sense of village religion). The making of drums has been secularized. That is, ceremonies that accompany their manufacture have been declared null and void and so ignored by Christians. Of course drums are always especially dedicated in church before being used there, but so is most other church bric-a-brac such as ceiling fans and floor carpets. The carved stations of the cross and the church linen can now come directly from Africa. The earth is the Lord's and everything in it too, and on this foundation Christianity is coming to grips with the external manifestations of African culture. Most of the literature on African theology and Christianity in Africa reviews this process.

In Ram Desai's *Christianity in Africa as Seen by Africans* (1962) many of these issues surfaced. Over and over again the statement is put: If Christianity is synonymous with Western culture and Western sensitivities then it is misplaced in Africa. Questions are still being raised, for,

> You may come to baptism with your African name.
> You may come to be married in African clothes.
> You may drum and even dance in church.
> But at the Eucharist
> can you use wine made of anything but grapes
> and bread which is made of wheat?
> These things do not grow in most parts of Black Africa.[5]

Does a ritual meal have to conform strictly to the normal diet of the people? What are the most important elements about the Eucharist, and are those jeopardized by what you actually eat and drink? Superficial as the acculturation discussion seems to be, it does ask for an explanation of the Eucharist in theological terms. Many more questions will be raised as these external adaptations are reviewed.

The report on a consultation of the Missiological Institute at Lutheran Theological College (Mapumulo, Natal, September 12–21, 1972) features some of these questions, as does Erasto Mugo's book, *African Response to Western Christian Religion* (East Africa Literature Bureau, 1975). Mugo undertakes a sociological analysis of African separatist religious and political movements in East Africa.

INCULTURATION

The process described as inculturation raises questions regarding the incorporation of African social structures and religious practices into Christianity. How can one be African and Christian at the same time? In this area we meet, for example, questions about the rites of passage, naming and other initiation ceremonies, as they confront Christian baptism and confirmation. However, inculturation discussions tend to focus on the humanizing effect of Christianity on communities. Thus Western Christians will point to the Christian command "thou shalt not kill" and the way that it has influenced legislation against the ritual killing of human beings and has introduced more respect for human-beings into Africa. These are sensitive areas, for it seems that what Christian theology gives with one hand, Christian practice and Christian peoples take away with the other. The process of inculturation as I understand it is still going on among all peoples of the world and has to continue until we all conform to the stature of humanity that is in Christ, that we may be presented blameless before God. The study undertaken by Sedos seeks to clarify this issue, while the Ecumenical Association of Third World Theologians' inclusion of the question of "Anthropological Poverty" in its study projects will, it is hoped, produce in-depth studies of Christ and culture on the African scene.

Indigenization

E. B. Idowu's use of the term *indigenization* is an attempt to demolish the artificial wall between acculturation and inculturation. Evolving terminology in one's native tongue to express novel experiences and hunches does not come easily; doing so in another's language cannot but be a matter of trial and error, especially if the emotions generated by the experiences are alien to the borrowed language. Idowu states the question in his book *Towards an Indigenous Church*:

Is Christianity not after all a European Institution which has no beneficial relevance for Nigerians, but which has nevertheless been imposed upon them as an engine of colonial policy by their European overlords? And if that is so, what is the need for Nigerians to continue to accommodate the imposition at this time of the day when they are wide awake to their independence as a nation, when the colonial structure which it served had collapsed under the impact of nationalism?" [Idowu 1965b, 1–2].

Idowu sees Christianity in Nigeria (and the rest of Africa too) as being on trial and reads off the charges, summing up in this way: "The question is crucial. If it is true that Christianity is a White man's cult, a kind of imperialistic witchcraft . . . its spell has now been broken; the magic . . . has lost its power" (Idowu 1965b, 2).

In the 1980s Christianity continues to hound the African's religious sensitivities. To indigenize Christianity, according to Idowu, is to work and pray for Christianity to shine in its own light and for the cosmic Christ to appear truly cosmic and the only Lord of his church (Ibid. 9-15). He devotes half of his book to the definition of indigenization, which he himself admits is an inelegant word, one that is not even in the *Concise Oxford Dictionary*. Idowu wrote from the Nigerian experience, which had produced the National Church of Nigeria, a neoreligious movement that "imitates the church in organization and cultus" but has nothing to do with the religion of the Christian church except that it aims at ousting it. In 1945 in the city of Benin, an ancient cultural and Christian center, the Arousa Church was active. It was modeled after the Roman Catholic Church, but was really a reformation of the primal religion of the Edo involving the ancient pantheon without symbolic representations of the divinities. This adoption of church structure by the primal religions is excluded from the term *indigenization* as Idowu presents it. Neither is a church indigenized by a change in its leadership from European to African.

By indigenization Idowu means that

the Church should bear the unmistakable stamp of the fact that [it] is the Church of God in Nigeria, not an outreach or colony of Rome, Canterbury or Westminster Central Hall, London or the vested interest of some European or American missionary board [Ibid. 11].

For Idowu indigenization covers the whole of the church's life, the language of the Bible and of evangelization, Christian literature, theology, liturgy, dress and vestments, and so on.

The theology of an indigenous church, the sort described by Idowu, cannot be a simple rewriting of European theology based on the European experience of the lordship of Christ. It will have to reflect the atmosphere of spiritual freedom experienced through being in Christ but living in Nigeria. It will have to reflect the preeminence and lordship of Christ over all things and thereby enable Christians to give undivided allegiance to Christ alone, whether they live in Nigeria or elsewhere.

Christian theology in Africa will become truly indigenous as it struggles with the question raised by C. H. Dodd: "Is the God of our redemption the same as the God of our creation?" To do this one cannot ignore the primal religions of Africa (Idowu 1956b, 25).

Idowu too speaks of "the pitfalls with which the way is un-doubtedly strewn in the process of indigenization." So the word "pitfalls" comes up again. These modern dogmaticians of West Africa—Idowu, Kato, and Baëta—are all steeped in the New Testa-ment tradition of salvation from sin. For Kato that line is clear and there can be no other. For Idowu our traditional religions belong to the sphere of God's saving acts among us; Baëta feels it is about time we started paying attention to the fruits of freedom from spiritual bondage. Of the three it is only Baëta who has seen the necessity of validating liberation theology. Idowu's concern for liberation from racism and cultural domination falls short of tak-ing into account the politicoeconomic shackles that cripple the African spirit, including the freedom to theologize. None of the three and to my knowledge few other African male theologians (with the outstanding exception of Sabelo Ntwasa and Basil Moore) have anything to say about sexism in the church in Africa (Moore 1973, 18–28).

For the Orthodox Churches sexism is another pitfall, as the debate on the implications of baptizing women into Christ goes on. They see the whole sexism discussion as a new form of heresy—they have their traditions (they say) and they are going to abide by them, come wind, come weather.[6] Young pastors in Sweden are against the ministry of ordained women.

These pitfalls—imaginary or real—should not prevent theologians in Africa and elsewhere from being open to what the Spirit is saying. It is clear that we all hear different things, but that has always been the case.

Marcion, in the second century, built up a canon of Christian Scriptures and systematized a definite theology. He struggled with some of the things that we still face. Is the God of creation the same as the God of redemption? How does one decide which of the many religious experiences that go into theology come from people who have stood in the Council of God? Those who condemned Marcion as a heretic were sure they had found the answers. Montanus, a heretic in his overemphasis on the presence of the Holy Spirit, did remind the "orthodox" theologians of Nicaea to append the words "and also the Holy Spirit" to their declaration of faith. The history of Christian theology shows that those who produced heterodox teaching did not always stray into pitfalls. If this were so we could have had no Lutherans and no Wesleyans.

Christian theology, pure and simple, is happening in the Third World. The attempt at a thousand qualifications all come from panic and uncertainty. The desire to be seen as orthodox or to nip heresy in the bud has stimulated much debate. We Christians are confronted with this fact: those who were for a long time content to be consumers of theology have begun to be producers of theology, and it is Christian theology. They are widening the panorama of symbols, heightening the colors of issues, and demanding commitment and action.

So I end this chapter as I began. Third World theology needs no other qualifying term except that it is theology from the underside of history, and African theology is nothing less than the theological insights that Christians in Africa are bringing to Christian theology. The challenges to theology in Africa may be specific to Africa in the details of the confrontation, but they are part of the challenges of our human realities as a whole. To treat them as exotic additions would be to sin against the Holy Spirit, and *that* would be heresy. We have to do theology, believing that when our honest labors are offered to God, God's holiness burns away the dross and allows the purity of the gold to shine, leading those who live in darkness to see a Great Light.

II

THEMES IN
AFRICAN THEOLOGY

6

Created and Redeemed

THE EXODUS EVENT

Reflection on the departure of the children of Israel from Egypt gives us valuable insight into the Judeo-Christian recognition of God at work and into theology generally. Creation and redemption, interwoven processes in which God is revealed, are seen by Christians following the Jewish heritage from the perspective of the exodus event. Dawn and light are often used as symbols of deliverance thus bringing together creation and exodus (see Is 8:20, 9:2, 33:2; Lam 3:23; Jn 8:12).

I begin with the exodus event, first, because it is in harmony with my own experience. Second, it is the deliverance from Egypt that made possible the whole Hebrew experience as a people who were God's special creation. The exodus event explains and interprets their history. The victory song led by Miriam (Exodus 15) rings authentically and spontaneously—just what a group of Fante women would have done after a breathtaking deliverance.

Sing to the Lord, for he has triumphed gloriously;
[because "he is indeed very high," *kiy ga'oh ga'ah*]
 . . . the horse and his rider he has thrown into the sea
(Ex 15:1).

Yahweh is indeed very high. As their history unfolded and the Hebrews began to recognize "the hand of God" in their realities and to understand the depths of God's liberative works, the Song of Moses was composed. God is powerful, God is glorious, God wins victories: they understood this liberative activity as the outcome of the nature of God as a caring God.

God was present in the conquest of Canaan and in the building of the nation and its temple. Israel saw itself as uniquely God's and the experience of sealing the covenant at Mount Sinai sealed this faith. From then on not just the community but individuals as well were believed to be unique in their relationship with Yahweh, and the affirmation is repeated throughout Scripture. "The Lord is my strength and my song, . . . my salvation" (Ps 118:14).

Yahweh is a warrior who crushes the enemy in order to deliver the oppressed, who cry for liberation. Yahweh enables them to build in glory. Yahweh brings glory out of nothingness. The priestly theologians of the Jews set down their version of the creation myth of their part of the world in terms of chaos and its resolution. Within the creation narrative is embedded the Hebrew experience of deliverance. The meaning of life and of the world for the community as well as for the individual was to be found in the God who delivers. Faced with suffering and death, the people cry out and their cry goes up to God: Save, Oh, Yahweh. He who delivered the children of Israel from Egypt, Daniel from the lions, and Jonah from the whale—why can't he deliver me? Africans forcibly taken to the Americas and those left to labor at home for the same oppressors adopted the Christian faith and joined in the Hebrew affirmation that Yahweh triumphs over chaos. This affirmation was submerged when Paul "spiritualized" the exodus (1 Cor 10:1-5). Redemption by Yahweh is limited to redemption from sin by Christ. The cry of the oppressed through the ages has often been either ignored or interpreted in terms of their personal sinfulness, thus letting-be the sinful structures that threaten to suffocate us all.

OUR BURDEN

In Africa, as we have seen, it is the experience of liberation from colonialism and the cry for this liberation that have stimulated theologies that struggle to be relevant to the realities of Africa. Indeed in the political struggles that led to independence the motif of the exodus from Egypt was a paradigm that played a key role as the charismatic leaders were cast in the image of Moses. In Ghana the struggle was seen as a march out of colonialism that would set the people on the road to freedom. The party anthem of the ruling Convention Peoples' Party was "Lead Kindly Light." It was indeed a revolution; the Ga women expressed it as "an about-face [that] has been shouted." Turn your back on the fleshpots of Egypt and face the struggles of the desert. The slogan of the party— Freedom—was a cry and a hope. In Kenya, the leader of the Mau Mau changed his name to "the light of Kenya," Jomo Kenyatta. Thus it is apposite to examine the theological content of the biblical exodus, to listen to what it has said and can say to Africa, as the nations struggle to be fully liberated from colonialism and from their internal misgoverning of themselves.

The traditional ordering of society placed its own burdens on the African people. So African theologians do not see the problem as one of captivity only to foreign nations. The task is not to retain and uphold tradition until the exile is over and a return and rebuilding can take place. In relation to traditional society one can still see the exodus as a paradigm, a departure from inflexibly ascribed positions whose hierarchical ordering was accepted as "natural" and permanent. Notwithstanding the fact that almost everybody cooperated and deviants were punished, it was an oppressive system to the extent that to opt out was to be cast out.

The colonial period was not much different. White leadership was imposed (especially in urban areas) and colonial officers administered the county without involving the people except for the few *akrakyefo* (clerks, civil servants) and *Ahenfo* (traditional rulers) who were co-opted to see that the white man's bidding was done. The exodus was to get out of all this. Independent movements in Africa were not seen as a return to a precolonial order; rather they were a fresh chance for new things to happen. The hope was that these new things would bring about more humanization; that is, bestow more dignity on the beings made in the image of God and called God's children.

Thus it was that the independent movements revived the recognition of charisma (placing it above birth) and applauded achievement (placing it above heritage) as the parameters by which to judge those assuming responsibility, especially as regards public office.[1] These leadership positions were not seen as permanent, and if "the Spirit of God left you" and you ceased to seek the well-being and dignity of the people, you ceased to be a leader. With the emergence of a new elite under this principle of charismatic leadership, our perennial coups d'etat were inaugurated. When charisma departs, despotism sets in and the people are moved to reject the person whom God had already rejected.[2]

LEAVING THE OLD BEHIND

The exodus is a well-rehearsed event, and in Africa it has not grown stale. Just as the Jews retold it and relived it every time they were in need of or were thankful for deliverance so do African Christians. It has become our story. It has ceased to be the exclusive story of the descendants of the *Habiru* and has become universally applicable to all peoples who believe in God the Creator, who saves from chaos. There follows a rereading of Exodus 1–3 (the situation of the Hebrews in Egypt) and 12:29–34 (the Tenth Plague) with special focus on the people who were caught up in a human predicament.

The children of Israel, an immigrant people, lived among the Egyptians. The leaders of Egypt began to feel threatened by their presence and took steps to curb their development. Under their new policy the Hebrews were forced to build for others. Life became unbearable under the hard and alienating labor, but the Hebrew population still grew, as happens often under oppressive and dehumanizing situations.

So the Egyptian authorities decided to control the Hebrew population by the most direct method: infanticide. Only females were to live since if males were allowed to survive they might join with invaders against the oppressive regime. The Hebrews groaned under the burden, and cried out to God (2:23–25). A number of Egyptian and Hebrew women buried their ethnic allegiances and took the side of God to frustrate the efforts of the Pharaoh and to promote life. Let's take a look at them.

The midwives were women who refused to be coopted by the oppressor. The narrator says it is because they were God-fearing.

They had skills which could be put to demonic use, but it seems they saw to the safe delivery even of Egyptian women. They must have been both compassionate and competent and were obviously full of wisdom.

Jochebed and Miriam were the mother and daughter who schemed day and night so that Moses might live. Their agony must have been beyond bounds. They, like the midwives, had to devise a way of getting around the oppressors' instructions. *Pharaoh's daughter* did exactly the opposite of what her father had decreed— she saved a Hebrew boy instead of destroying him. Miriam, the intelligent sister, dutifully watching her baby brother (a familiar African scene), was at hand to see that Moses was returned to his own mother.

Moses, the charismatic leader who emerged from this situation of oppression, alienation, and dehumanization, began by treating the Pharaoh with dignity: he talked to him—as one who would heed the voice of God, one who would respond to God. Moses began with negotiations; he asked leave for the people to go on a retreat to meet their God. Instead of the situation getting better, it took a turn for the worse. The accredited leaders of the children of Israel (the tax-masters) took the side of the oppressors and agreed to carry on their assignment of making sure the Hebrews were economically productive. They must have suffered the dilemma of the co-opted, a situation well illustrated in Africa's colonial history. They had to weigh evil against evil and try to discover the lesser evil; they chose physical existence under inhuman conditions to death. Perhaps they saw nothing to die for! The people too were ambivalent about their liberator Moses, who claimed to be acting on the instructions of the God of their ancestors, Yahweh. When they experienced setbacks and obstacles on their way to freedom they asked, "Were there no graves in Egypt?" They too had nothing to die for, not even the name of God who comes to save. Life for these migrant people had been reduced to mere existence, and the courage to be the People of God had almost left them. Although they were landless, the promise of getting a homeland and becoming a people did not excite them—the fleshpots of Egypt were too attractive. They found it difficult to exchange a certain present for an uncertain future.

God does not rescue people in spite of themselves. The people had to be fully involved in their own liberation, women and men alike. Hence there appear in this story of liberation villains, heroines, heroes, oppressors, and oppressed—those whose orientation is toward the saving work of God and those who operate according to the power they wield as human beings.

Moses proved himself a leader even before he was called, attempting according to his light to bring reconciliation among the oppressed. Once a privileged member taken from the oppressed to enjoy the favors of the palace, he became the challenger of the authority of the Pharaoh over the Hebrew people. He understood from his experience on Mount Sinai that the destiny of the children of Israel was to be servants of Yahweh, not of Pharaoh. He had earlier renounced the privileges of the elite in order to identify with the oppressed and had for a time been a refugee from Egyptian law. After his encounter on the mountain he was to use the skills he had acquired by his education and vocation to confront the powers. But Moses could never have liberated the people without their cooperation. His credentials were questioned, not only by Pharaoh but also by his own people: "Who made you a prince and a judge over us?" (Ex 2:14).

Pharaoh's image is that of the oppressor. He is totally self-centered. He cannot see himself without the Hebrew slaves, portraying the psychology of those who say "I am because I dominate" (Zoe-Obianga 1983, 72; Taylor 1963, 85). The powerful never let go because they cannot exist as entities in themselves; they are nothing if they do not have others to trample under their feet or to look down upon. They know no other life and therefore have to do all they can to retain the situation that gives them their dominant role; hence they are dehumanized and they dehumanize others. In the exodus event as narrated, every round of negotiations resulted in further hardships for the oppressed. The powerful and dominant, like the Pharaoh, only let go when they are directly affected by the calamities caused by their actions and decisions. It was only when Pharaoh lost his firstborn that he "let go." In the end, in trying to safeguard his way of life, he lost even his physical existence as an individual. The sufferings of the people he ruled, both natives and immigrants, did not move him; neither did the disharmony that afflicted the rest of creation in his domain (Croatto 1981, 23–24).

Pharaoh's action was motivated in his eyes by his desire to

safeguard the security of his domain; he was being prudent. It was this political sagacity that dictated the policy to wear the Hebrews down with labor, to use their own people to subjugate them. Do everything to break their backs and their spirits. All this he commanded out of his fear of losing power and prestige. Oppressors are only fulfilled if there are others they can oppress. *Ohuruye ti mu mpa mmogya,* "the tsetse fly must always have blood in its head, or it ceases to be a tsetse fly."

Yahweh heard the crying and the groaning and called to mind (Ex 6:5) the covenant made with Abraham, Isaac, and Jacob. God saw and knew the misery of the people (Ex 2:23–25). Deliverance from Egypt was linked to the covenant—not only that covenant made with "the ancestors" but also that covenant made with the people on Mount Sinai, which made all the people responsible for its keeping and beneficiaries of its blessings. But who is Yahweh? Moses, Pharaoh, the people—all asked this question.

The Yahwist narrator's answer is that Yahweh is El Shaddai, the fighting God, who is in a holy war against oppression from whatever quarter. Yahweh will use power to rout the oppressor (Ex 6:2–3, 7:4). Yahweh's power is the power to save. In the exodus event Israel experienced Yahweh's promise to make them a people, to give them land, and to be God to them. Yahweh becomes the reason for Israel's existence; they describe themselves by God, they are the people of God, not just the children of Abraham or Israel. It is God who makes their nationhood possible.

African Christian theologians, though operating from a religiously pluralistic context, claim that it is the same One God of all creation who operates in Africa as elsewhere and who is recognized in the religions of the continent (Pobee 1976a, 129–142). Laying claim to the Jewish—Christian heritage of the exodus becomes a matter of faith in the One God, Creator and Liberator. The oppressed in the exodus story were immigrants; in Africa's history it is the oppressor who is the immigrant, and in Africa oppression takes many forms.[3]

Multiple Burdens

People live on their own soil in Africa, but are exploited by immigrants, as in a situation of colonialism. Others live on their own soil but are virtually working for overlords overseas. This situation of neocolonialism exists throughout Africa, for planting coffee and cocoa are close to the forced labor of building pyramids. Oppressive situations are created by sheer self-seeking and love of power. There are those people who suffer under the above oppressions and are also treated as minors, whose manner of contributing is dictated by tradition, not aptitude or need.

These situations are the most alienating because people come to accept what is said of them. They become strangers to their own potential and cannot imagine any other way of organizing society or their personal lives. The norm of operation is that "things-as-they-are" is the best way. This situation calls for *metanoia*, a hundred and eighty degree reorientation toward the person as the child of God and the whole people as the people of God.

DECODING THE EXODUS

I cannot help but hear the promise and the call to the adventure of freedom in the exodus story. In every situation of alienation some escape the internalization syndrome. They recognize that a situation that prevents one from full human responsibility cannot be natural. This realization informs rebellion against the so-called normal, traditional, natural way. It stimulates the crying and the groaning. The individual Hebrew was liberated in order to get on the road to fulfillment. But the exodus is not so much personal as it is political. Pharaoh made a sociopolitical decision. His consideration had to do with cheap labor and state security; he neglected the fact that the personal growth and the well-being of two ethnic groups (Egyptian natives and Habiru immigrants) would both be affected by his decision. When God saves, God saves totally. God purges the sociopolitical chaos in order to provide an atmosphere within which the fullness of humanity can flower.

We also see in the exodus story the various uses of power. Power in the sense of ability or authority to make things happen or to prevent them from happening may be said to be neutral. God's power in the exodus was creative: the power to save, to create space in which people could grow. But power can be put to negative use—in the hands of Pharaoh it was. That kind of power is to be repudiated and broken. In the exodus we see also how God uses the skills and willingness of human beings and even their social status to bring about liberation—the daughter of Pharaoh, the midwives, the eloquence of Aaron, and the long association of Moses with the court of Pharaoh.

In Africa human initiatives in the liberation process are acknowledged. The charismatic leaders are recognized as God-sent and the people put their hands in theirs. The pioneer leaders were treated as God's gift to the suffering people. In some parts of Africa, the process of political liberation was conceived and described in religious terms. Most conspicuous was Kwame Nkrumah's Convention People's Party (CPP) with its anthem "Lead Kindly Light." God was seen as being in the situation because the situation was liberative. Foreign rule was to be overthrown in order to enable the Africans to build up a new society. Critics were to denounce this combination of the political and the religious as blasphemous. Certain interpretations of the Young Pioneer Movement led to uneasiness that Ghana might be putting Nkrumah in the place of God or at least had embarked upon his apotheosis.[4] This does no more than illustrate the interpretation of the process of colonial liberation as a religious experience. Neither a Christian church closely associated with the foreign government nor the coopted educated elite could be trusted. Like Pharaoh's taskmasters, both were identified with the oppressive regime.

When Nkrumah's statue was erected it bore one of his supposedly blasphemous utterances: "Seek ye first the political kingdom and everything else will be added." Is the "political kingdom" always opposed to the "kingdom of God"? In the political kingdom that Ghana sought the first were to be the last and the people were to express their wishes through the Party organization right from village level. Another "religious" aspect of the movement was that it was seen as a march: a people going in the wrong direction had turned around, led by the warrior whom God had sent, but above all led by the Light of God. God had sent a Moses to get us out from under the burdens of colonialism and to make us a free nation with new opportunities for a fuller life. The exodus event is read as a call to freedom; it is the beginning of a process, just as the independence celebrations and the five-year development plans of Ghana are a call to the future.

Where church leaders read the independence struggle as a work of God, Christians had no problems with reconciling nationalism with Christianity. But in some places the missionaries, both black and white, read and reread Romans 13 to their congregations without any reference to Revelation 13. Only the status quo was seen as showing God's presence. Initially the leaders of the independence movements were seen as troublemakers. They opened the eyes of people to the realities in their situations. But the leaders who confused the call to the desert with the possession of the promised land were bound to bring disillusionment to the people.

The exodus happened, the motley group of Habiru was changed into a nation under the hand of God. New life and new perspectives are possible if God is in the situation. The conclusion of the anti-independence missionaries was to refuse to see God working through the human agency that emerged among Africans. Whether one looks at the present politico-economic instability or repression of African countries from the perspective of neocolonialism or that of exploitation by nationals, Africans have tasted liberation and are aware of the need to strive through the desert, through a state of continuing liberation from one oppressor or another. Whether Africans need new skills for running the courts of justice or new methods of economic survival or even wars with the forces that prevent entry into the promised land, the sea has already been crossed.

A look at South Africa and its black theologians reveals an awareness of the exodus as God's "No" to chaos and exploitation. The "Pharaohs" of South Africa have the same arguments as did the Pharaoh of Egypt, only they are not honest enough to say so. It is evident that the heart of the oppressor is hardened. Instead of becoming aware of the sin of the situation, the oppressors simply lay plans to oppress and intimidate them more, those whose cry has gone up to God.

The exodus event, attested to outside Hebrew literature, is a gift to the oppressed.[5] The meaning Israel found in this episode has been appropriated and reapplied by others in similar situations. Those who have known no sociopolitical and economic colonization can afford the luxury of spiritualizing the event. That too is legitimate if one can learn the meaning of sin and the implications of personal involvement in communal sin.

When oppressed peoples meet obstacles, the event of the exodus reassures them. Every triumph on the way evokes the Song of Miriam. Thus the journey to the promised land is a journey undertaken in the spirit of doxology. The oppressed become a people empowered by the presence of God-with-them and like Miriam they continually recognize God as the author of their success. The religious base of life in Africa enables us to read our history as "sacred" history. *Gye Nyame,* "Except God," is one of the pillars of the primal religion of the Ghanaian, for without God nothing holds together.[6] God interferes here and now, making salvation-liberation one activity of God. We believe in providence and therefore are ready to see God in daily happenings, whether they concern the individual or the community.

7

Except God

CREATION AS LIBERATION

Without God nothing holds together; nothing has any meaning. It is God, *Bọrebọre*, who fashioned the universe (*bọ adze*), who called Being into being.[1] To read Genesis 1 is to call to mind the universal intuition that the universe, all in it, and all that happens in it has a Designer and Maker. "Things" are not here by chance, and one expects an answer to the call "is anyone in charge here?" In Genesis, God "delivers" the universe from chaos, just as out of compassion God delivered the Habiru from Egypt. The narrative does not pretend to be a history of origins or a scientific explanation of what is. It is an attempt to say who God is, to affirm that chaos is contrary to the nature of God, and that the universe came into being out of the "pain of God."

In the creation stories of the Mesopotamian civilization, Marduk (the Good Force) rescues the world from the belly of Tiamat (the dragon, the Evil Force), or uses her body as material for making the heavens and the earth. The Hebrew narrative is one of several such stories that were told in eastern Mediterranean lands (Shapiro and Hendricks 1981, xxi, 119). The Hebrew version is unique in that it tells of God's transforming a chaotic situation by a creative act that rescued the "earth" from formlessness—*Tohu wa Bohu*, "emptiness and formlessness." This is how the priestly theologian of

Genesis 1 perceives God. Creation was a deliberate act of God, who acted freely to bring meaning to what otherwise would have been "tractless waste and emptiness" (*JB* 15). Out of the darkness over the deep comes an orderly succession of light and dark. Yahweh was totally in control, and in a neat six-day operation all was complete and God could rest; the universe had been given a (new) beginning and the earth began its individual existence in the context of God's ordered creation.

The second narrative (Gn 2:4–25) puts more "matter" into the event. The Earth Creature is made from earth, and the serpent sets itself up to oppose Yahweh like a dragon from the Mesopotamian myths. As in those narratives the serpent caused humanity's mortality. (In the myth the herb of rejuvenation given to Gilgamesh by Uta-Napishtim was devoured by the serpent who left its old skin behind).[2] Several biblical references echo the Mesopotamian stories in which God steps into a situation to redeem matter from formlessness. Marduk struggled to make the good heaven and the good earth out of the body of the evil Tiamat, but the Hebrew Yahweh of the priestly view simply calls into being, transforms nonexistence into existence. The Yahwist writer preserves bits of the primeval struggle found in other versions.

The history of the Jews is the paradigm of transformation. In their collective memory and national experience God transformed a heterogeneous group of individuals and tribes into a nation under God by the Sinai covenant. This transformation is repeated in the lives of individuals who cry to God.[3] Similarly, an Akan folktale tells of Ananse Kokroko (the Great Spider, a linguistic device employed to avoid using God's personal name, Nyame), who was aware of constant fighting between "Half and Half." Ananse Kokroko steps in, gets hold of the two, slams them together, and out of two made one whole human being. This is one of the few creation stories the Akan have; in it we see God's direct involvement in order to transform a situation of disharmony.

According to the elaborate creation myth of the Yoruba, Olodumare fashioned the earth and all that it contains through the use of agents, but closely supervised the process personally. By whatever process, when humans think of their earthly home, they perceive God at work. I do not know of any primal worldview of Africa that leaves our existence to chance. God is at work making a new thing out of the chaotic old. It is interesting to note that during the Habiru's days in the desert even the serpent was transformed into a salvific agent (Nm 21:9; Jn 3:14).

The creation story of Genesis 1 is about the redemption that God brings to our chaotic world. It is a theological statement affirming that God responds to situations. God, as the Hebrew and the Akan perceive, is not the Impassible One of Greek philosophy. God is affected and is not immune to mutability. In fact God is plainly vulnerable. It is this co-passionate (compassionate) and "vulnerable" God that Christians see in Christ. God so *loved* that God *sent*. John 3:16 tells of the suffering love of God; the same love that conquered chaos pities the human condition and sends help. God so suffered with our suffering humanity and our suffering world that God did something about the situation: While we were yet afar off . . . God looked out for us (Lk 15:20). God turned in our direction: "As a father pities his son, so the Lord pities those who fear him" (Ps 103:13)[4]. One of the unique contributions of Christianity to religion is the doctrine that the messiah who suffered is certainly the very image of the suffering God. God's creative and redemptive powers flow out of this suffering love.

In the creation narratives, one may trace the theme of redemption/liberation/salvation in Genesis 2-3. To correct the state of alone-ness and to create a community, God makes two sexes out of the Earth-Creature Adam.[5] Even when mistrust leads human beings to take their destiny into their own hands and to attempt to do without God, God still has compassion, cares and provides "a covering" for the shame-evoking nakedness of the woman and the man.

Among the Igbo of Nigeria, to be creative is to turn the power of evil, sin, and suffering into the power of love. When things are not going well in a community, in order to restore harmony and mutuality of existence, this African community requires artists to camp together, to work together to heal the society by their sacrifice. The creativity of the artists is the sacrifice required for righting wrongs in the community. The artists fashion a model of a whole community and all that they have in a house (*Mbari*), and the house and its artifacts are left as a sacrifice, which will renew the community (Okparocha 1977). (For the Kikuyu of Kenya the word *Mbari* means "clan" [Desai 1962, 101].) The artist symbolically recreates the clan in its pristine state through artifacts and the result is salutary for the real clan. It becomes once again a wholesome people in a wholesome community. This symbolic "new creation" out of a chaotic old appears in the Bible in the stories of the flood, the replenishing of the world, and the apocalyptic new creation of Revelation: "Behold, I make all things new" (Rv 21:5.) Christianity believes this new creation has already begun with the coming of the Christ.

OWNER OF THE EARTH

The creation narrative underlines the fact that the universe belongs to God who created it and that there is an interdependence of God's world and God's people. The story is a challenge and a judgment on how we run the world in our day. God speaks to humanity and humanity has the ability to respond to God. Made in God's image, we are expected to be God-like.

From this perspective we hear the narrator telling of the existing disharmonies of our world: disharmony in nature, caused by human excesses and irresponsibility (Gn 3,4,6). To tell this tale of woe, the narrator begins with a scene in which God is "absent" (Gn 3:1-7). The woman talks about God with the Serpent (the opponent of God); the man stands by not taking part in this God-talk (theological disputation) but also completely forgetful of his responsibility to God who had commanded that the fruit of that tree was not to be eaten. The woman, restating and interpreting God's command, puts the case even stronger than God had, adding that the tree must not even be touched. "You shall not eat of the fruit of the tree . . . , neither shall you touch it, lest you die" (Gn 3:3). This is a rabbinic device called hedging the Torah. But knowing the law does not necessitate obedience.[6] An analysis of God's intentions begun, the woman proceeded to look to what she thought was her self-interest. She came to the conclusion that the reason for keeping away from the tree was simply obedience to God. But why obey? She decided to experiment and persuaded the man, the unquestioning collaborator who acquiesced to the demands of another who claimed to have thought through the whole issue and weighed all its aspects.

The narrator, looking at his own society and perceiving various levels of disintegration and disharmony, tells this persuasive and "true" story: we do make a mess of our world when we ignore God's voice and mis-use both the natural order and our human companions in the process of seeking our interests. The earth is the Lord's, not ours, and hence there is a limit to how far we can bend it to suit ourselves. Contravening the laws that hold it together cannot but result in a return to the chaos from which it was created.

The cynicism of the snake, the distrust of the woman, and the apathy of the man are all well-known elements in the generation and maintenance of chaos in the context of the world within which the story was being told as they are in ours today. Nevertheless the redemptive effort is continued as the woman continues to work in today's world for the mutuality decreed by God and denied by the man. The male principle in the world, however, instead of seeking community attempts to forestall being an unquestioning follower by swinging to the other end of the pendulum and becoming a being whose power to be depends on the non-being of others. Neither domination nor acquiescence in human relations can make for a healthy community. Only participation will do it; hence the emphasis on *Koinonia* in the Christian community. The Hebrew narrator, being a man of his times, puts into the mouth of God words that validate the status quo, stating them as if God were decreeing what ought to be rather than stating what becomes inevitable when we refuse to live *coram Deo*. In the scene that tells of the consequences of disobedience (Gn 3:14–19) God is present. God returned to the scene created by the germination of the seeds of chaos, which had flowered into distrust, disintegration, and disharmony—chaos.

When God returned, cynicism, distrust, and apathy were declared illogical in divine-human relationship. Far from sanctioning our evil ordering of society, this myth is a judgment on what is—our refusal to observe limits, an outcome of the yearning to be independent of God. To be totally dependent on God, we have to have absolute trust in God. The Hebrew answer to the question "Is there any one in charge here?" is Yes! God is in charge and God gives us what is for our good. Cynicism in our relationship to God cannot make for a healthy human community. Our community with God depends on our complete trust in God. We experience a chaotic world of human creation, ecological disruption, and the absence of *Shalom*—the groaning of the whole creation (Rom 8:22–23). By magic, science, and technology we claim the "right" to use and misuse the earth, assuming that it is humanity that is in charge here. Where the human being (a-theistic) is in charge instead of people(s) growing into communities, a hierarchical system of domination exists, blame is apportioned where situations are the creation of communal irresponsibility, and the desire for community is blatantly exploited.

In Africa as elsewhere a literal reading of the creation narratives has stifled the theological content and buried the chance for real reflection. A rereading of Genesis 1-3 from the perspective of the liberated children of Israel conveys other messages. The narrative, far from sanctioning what is, is a judgment on the world as we run it. It exposes the sin in patriarchy as well as that in matriarchy. Hierarchy that undermines community and ignores individuals' ability to contribute is condemned. The story exposes our refusal to observe limits set by the God who frees from chaos and who is the only lawgiver. We would gladly put limits on others if that made us feel fulfilled, and yet to have dominion over the earth involves being disciplined. The narrative shows our unbelief in our verbal acknowledgment that God knows what we need. It calls us back to God in our original shameless nakedness, vulnerability, and mutuality. It calls for mutual respect, respect for the toughness and tenderness that is latent or patent in both women and men. Above all the narrative talks of the love of God for a recalcitrant world.

The theme of love that goes to the rescue is illustrated throughout the gospels in stories of healing and teaching. Luke's story of the loving father is especially illustrative of God's love. The father suffers, waiting anxiously, straining and scanning the horizon, waiting and longing to give the child the good news of his acceptance back into the family. This image together with that of the caring shepherd and the lost coin presents us with a God who suffers to give us the chance of a second birth. Saving us from ourselves, God effects our exodus, thus beginning our re-creation. Our problem is that we are not sheep, but moral agents, able to say No to God. So neither wins and God bears the burden of waiting longingly for us: "Behold, I stand at the door and knock" (Rv 3:20). "I will take you for my people, and I will be your God" (Ex 6:7). "You shall remember that you were a slave in Egypt" (Dt

16:12). More than this God actually searches for us and suffers until the community is complete.

A theology divorced from ethical demands would have little relevance in Africa. The exodus theme in Africa poses not only a question of liberation but one of "what shall we *do* to be saved?" For we shall not live the lives of a people of God if we only say "Lord, Lord" and we do not do what the Lord tells us (Lk 6:46). It is to highlight the necessity for an ethic of a redeemed people that African theologians need to review christology. When this has been done it will become clearer what it means to say: "Believe in the Lord Jesus, and you will be saved, you and your household" (Acts 16:31). The word that needs to be heard on this continent is the plan to redeem all that has been created by God. Salvation for an elite who have no responsibility to the community at large is contrary to the meaning of the Christ-event. For it is the One God without whom there is no existence who has accomplished our salvation in Christ.

8

Jesus Saves

The religious background to these studies is the primal religion of Africa and of Judaism. What we in Africa have traditionally believed of God and the transcendent order has shaped our Christianity. But that is only part of the story. Islam strides shoulder to shoulder with Christianity in Africa; the relationship of the two calls for serious consideration. Religious maturity, traditional hospitality to the stranger, and the sacredness of blood ties have enabled the adherents of these two faiths to accept the other's right to exist and in the family context to share each other's festivals. A practical dialogue has been initiated and goes on steadily. Nevertheless a situation of uneasy peace is sometimes made volatile by the extremist elements on both sides. The Christian side can have a Bible-centered, Christian-centered worldview that ignores all other aspects of the revelation of God. A religious "cold war," a war of minds, of ideas and beliefs, and even of styles of life and spirituality based on these two religions results. Theological dialogue has so far taken the form of two parallel monologues.

In such a situation, one needs to discover approaches to christology that will compel even those who claim to be without religion to pause and consider the Christ. The Christ in the popular theology of Africa is above all the one who saves. The "slogan," or affirmation, "Jesus saves" is written large on the minds and hearts of African Christians, and in Nigeria, literally written on buttons, on cars and walls. What does it mean, what does it imply? The answer to this question should be not a metaphysical analysis of what it means to be truly God and truly human but rather the christological quest of our times. Proclaiming the divinity of Christ is in the dimension of faith, but his lordship over life is clear from the style of life he lived. His total dependence upon God's power and love demands that one give that style of life a trial as being the perfect salvific life.[1] What are the salvific implications of his death and resurrection, especially in the context of Islam? What does his humanity mean in view of sexism and racism? These are the questions I bring to christology.

SALVATION AND LIBERATION

The *Agyenkwa*, the one who rescues, who holds your life in safety, takes you out of a life-denying situation and places you in a life-affirming one. The Rescuer plucks you from a dehumanizing ambiance and places you in a position where you can grow toward authentic humanity. The *Agyenkwa* gives you back your life in all its wholeness and fullness.

Who Needs a Savior?

Research into the phenomenon of religious conversion in Africa shows evidence of both spiritual and material struggles that prompted people to adopt Christianity. Those two struggles cannot be divorced, one from the other. Our worship of nature and our refusal to examine what we call natural, the selective beneficence implied in ethnic morality, our confusion of pluralism with sectionalism, our worship of elitism and neglect of peoples' participation, our refusal to deal with corruptive influences and practices, our worship of patriarchy and hierarchy—these should make all of us seekers after salvation. It is apposite to observe therefore that cries for salvation in the Old Testament mirror cries from the African continent. Even a word-study approach to the faith will illustrate this.

If one studies the Old Testament with the knowledge of the primal worldview of Africa and an awareness of the political and sociological realities that are shaping Africa as part of one's critical equipment, many similarities surface. The primal cry for salvation (*yeshuah*) is taken up in the New Testament and salvation is declared by Christianity to be in Christ.[2] This I believe is the reason for the continued attraction of Christianity to Africans, in spite of the negative burdens associated with its carriers. The Christ of Christianity touches human needs at all levels, and Africans are but ordinary members of the human race feeling the need for salvation. I choose only two of the felt needs that show Africa's readiness to accept salvation through Jesus Christ as Savior and Redeemer.

The Warrior-Savior of the Hebrew Scriptures

Yahweh, who fought Israel's battles against human enemies, was called Yahweh Sabaoth, the commander of the large array of forces. In Asante military terminology, Yahweh would have been called the *Tufohene*, the one who manages the logistics of the military, both physically and spiritually, and who actually directs the battles, fighting alongside his people. When the Israelites called God by the praise-name Sabaoth, they were referring to actual experiences of "God-at-war." God, the Savior from the rigors of battle, was a reality containing and eliminating actual enemies in literal battles. The salvation (Hebrew root word *Yasha'*) wrought by God was felt immediately in military and political terms. The military orders given to Israel's combatants were to prepare to fight, "for the Lord your God is he that goes with you, to fight for you against your enemies, to give you the victory" (Dt 20:1–4); if they are attacked, Yahweh will conquer the enemies (Dt 28:7).

In the narratives dealing with the conquest of Canaan, no victory was won without God. When the Philistines molested the Israelites, they called upon Yahweh to save them (1 Sm 7). Yahweh was, in the experience of Israel, the One who gives victory. In the language of the Akan, a people that had experienced long years of ethnic conflicts, *Osagyefo*, the one who saves in the battle, became a praise-name of God. Hence also the *Fantse* (Christian) lyrics that give God the praise-name *Osabarima*, the Great Warrior, the Lord of the Battle, literally, the Man of War. *Dǫmkuyin* in the song below is the best word to express Yahweh's praise-name, Sabaoth.

God leads the battle against oppressive forces. Let us give God thanks.

Wọmfa ndaase mma hẹn Hene o
Wọmfa ntonton mma Dọmkuyin
Waadan hẹn *hell* ato hẹn *heaven* o
Ọsabarima e
Yẹdawo ase a ọsa o.

Bring thanks to our King.
Bring praise to the Brave General
Who has turned our hell to heaven.
Savior of the Battle
We cannot thank you enough.

In the Christian lyrics, however, the spiritualization of life's battles is already in evidence. We bring thanks to God who has led our feet from the path that leads to hell onto that which lead to heaven. In the same lyric God is described as our Great Friend (*Adamfo Adu*) and Guarantor (*Okyirtaafo*). But even in this, one can see faith expressed in the God who transforms the experience of "hell" as the Christians had known it into "heaven" as they were beginning to experience it in the transformation of their primal and innate faith in God. The fact remains, nevertheless, and carries conviction for the African, that it is Yahweh who promises through Isaiah: "I will contend with those who contend with you" (Is 49:25). It is Yahweh who will smite the ruthless and the wicked (Is 11:3–5).

Salvation as the overcoming of external physical enemies in war does not preclude the inner battle against evil inclinations. For as Paul was to say later, the battle must be waged against the unseen powers (Eph 6:10–20). The fact that all human beings need the salvation of God from these powers does not prevent God from saving those who need salvation on both scores, for Yahweh Sabaoth liberates all who cry to him (Is 19:16–25). This is a remarkable view of God, showing that "exodus" does not belong only to one nation or people called Israel. "When they cry to the Lord because of oppressors we will send them a Savior, and will defend and deliver them" (Is 19:20).[3]

Our Reconciliation

In Yahweh all peoples will be reconciled because they will all come under one rule, that of Yahweh. The salvation that Christ brought is in line with this, for not only does he unite us all in himself but also in him we are at one with God.

This ministry of reconciliation to and in God is a key Christian interpretation of the Christ-event within Jewish-Christian salvation history. Jesus, in the Christian understanding, is the Christ, God's own "chosen instrument for our salvation." The name he bears, Jesus, is the hellenized version of the Hebrew name Yeshuah (Joshuah), but the situation he was sent to respond to contained elements beyond those of the period of the conquest associated with his namesake of the Hebrew Scriptures. Israel was a conquered nation living in captivity, not in Egypt, Assyria, or Babylon, but right in the very land God gave it. Israel had fallen under Roman colonial rule; the people were free to worship Yahweh and keep the Law as long as neither conflicted with Roman rule. In the midst of political and social oppression, we cannot forget that on the personal level individuals may still be plagued by feelings of estrangement from God. When large issues of national economy are being considered, it is often the case that the welfare of people as persons becomes obscured.

The debate over whether Jesus forgave sins before healing physical ills or vice versa exists because we create a dichotomy between the elements of human well-being. The human being is still an integrated person in Africa, the private and the political cannot be separated. Jesus exposed the structures of oppression that operated from temple and synagogue, those inherent in the interpretations of the Law of God and of what it means to be a people of God. Jesus worked for the soundness of persons and structures both religious and social.

Just as in the Hebrew Scriptures, Yahweh rescued people from childlessness and disease, famine and fire, from flood and from the deep sea, from disgrace and humiliation, so we find Jesus in the New Testament snatching women and men away from all domination, even from the jaws of death. He redeems by a strong hand all who are in the bondage of sin and who manifest their being in the service of sin by exploiting their neighbors. Today salvation has come to this house, Jesus told Zacchaeus (Lk 19:1-10), after a speech that echoes John the Baptist's preaching on the imminence of the Kingdom of God.

The One Who Redeems Us

The images of the Warrior and of the Liberator are companion images; they give us hope for space in which to be truly human. The Liberator will set us free through the process of redemption. The imagery of God in Christ as Redeemer is one that speaks clearly to Africa. In primal societies the *ponfo*, the one who pays back a loan for someone in debt, is appreciated and revered. "Redeeming" is also experienced through the custom of shaving off the hair of the widow and children at the death of husband and father. If they wish to keep their hair they have to "buy it back" by paying a sum of money. Surely for those who do not want to be shorn the one who enables them or allows them to "redeem" their hair shows them sympathy and consideration. In several Fanti hymns the "Great Redeemer" (Jesus Christ) is called *Ponfo Kese* (see Lv 25:47-50). Christians see themselves as having been taken away from the slavery of a lifestyle that was painful to God to one that makes them the family of God.

In the early period of evangelization in Africa south of the Sahara, which also coincided with the dying days of the slave trade, African Christians experienced redemption in its most literal form and therefore gave their lives to Christ. "To redeem," then, is as much an African concept as it is a Jewish one. Africans passing into Christianity are bound to carry with them these primal connotations.

While researching Jaba religion, Kato had occasion to explain to his home congregation why he was studying the religion they had left behind. He reports:

> They were all happy to know that all I can see in Jaba religion is a recognition of the craving after the Supreme Being, a search for reality in life, but at the same time a flight from God the Creator and Redeemer [Kato 1975, 38].

He went on to explain that "the beliefs of African traditional religions only locate the problem" but that "the practices point away from the solution." He then affirmed that "the incarnate risen Christ alone is the answer" (Kato 1975, 38).

The congregation, he said, was relieved. My relief is limited. First, note that Kato does not specify the *crucified* Christ. If he did one could ask whether all religious practices in the primal religions, including sacrifice, point away from the solution to our innate feeling of alienation from our true be-ing and the source of all Being.

Kato concedes at least that the primal religion of the Jaba does "locate the problem." It would have been helpful if he had gone on to find out the type of solutions envisaged in this view and whether they could be described as "salvation." That may have aided our understanding of salvation in Christ as understood by the Jaba. As it is, Kato begins with a "definition" of what it means "to be saved in the Judaeo-Christian sense." This he says "presupposes the lost condition from which salvation or deliverance is needed. What one is saved from determines the nature of Salvation" (Kato 1975, 38)

Since, according to Kato, the Jaba have "a wrong conception of sin" it was very easy to see how they also have a "wrong view of salvation." According to him all cries for political liberation and humanization have nothing to do with salvation, for salvation has to do exclusively with "eternal redemption from sin" (Ibid.). One is tempted to ask: What is sin? But crucial as this is I do not intend to deal with it as a separate theme. Suffice it to say that all that prevents us from living a life of absolute trust in God, living out the values of God's kingdom, is sin. It alienates us from God and from one another and turns the world God pronounced good into a veritable hell from which God is absent and in which we live as if we are neither seen nor heard by God.

Liberating Israel from slavery in Egypt was a salvific act born out of God's grace (Ex 15:13). This is what makes the historic exodus so fascinating. It is clear from that political deliverance that the redemption of a community from unjust systems is not outside God's providence, that what God found necessary to do for Israel God has found necessary to do for the colonized peoples of Africa, and is doing for those held in bondage inside Africa.

This however is not the whole content of the rich store of redemption imagery in the Old Testament. Africa experiences realities from which nations and individuals daily cry to be redeemed.

Some of these are like the experience of God's people Israel.

Salvation discussions that focus exclusively on giving satisfactions (*mpata*) to the injured honor of God and on redemption by the blood of Christ tend to lead to debates that leave the sinner and the slave as spectators.[4] Moreover to redeem is not only to buy back. The marketplace terminology associated with redemption is not to be allowed to overshadow God's action of taking off our chains so that we may be free to be fully human. God snatches us away, separates us from the oppressive environment, breaks off unjust relationships, and tears down dehumanizing structures (Ps 35:17, 136:24; Dn 6:27-28).

To attempt a comprehensive survey of the situation from which people are redeemed by God is not possible here. Neither can I refer to the rich images and vocabulary of deliverance in the Hebrew Scriptures. I suggest a few in a summary fashion only.

• Deliverance of nation from nation (Jer 31:11; Mi 4:10; 2 Sm 7:23)

• Deliverance from national sin (Ps 44:26, 130:8)

• Deliverance of individuals from other people(s) (2 Sm 4:9)

• Deliverance from dehumanization (Jb 5:15; Is 45:15,21; Ps 72:2), from the poverty that makes people sell themselves to others

• Deliverance from personal actions that cause disrupture in the relations with others and with God (Ps 51)

• God provides events to turn back to right religion those who have been lured into idolatry (2 Kgs 10:18-27).

Deliver us, liberate us and make a new nation of us; renew our humanity after the pattern inherent in you. Redemption often includes the sense of rescue (*Yasha'*). God gives safety by rescuing the bankrupt from the hands of the violent (Jb 5:15). God rescues from death, from murderers and persecutors, from all evil. God saves the fugitive (and there are many refugees in and from Africa). In wartime God rescues (*Padah*) from the stroke of the sword; God rescues from all troubles (Jb 5:8-16).

Psalm 72 carries the message of peace that God defends the poorest and saves the children of those in need. God rescues from the hands of the greedy and callous sheep, and will judge between sheep and sheep. So Ezekiel warns the fat sheep who, not content to graze in good pastures, trample down the rest (34:17-22). To bring renewed vigor to the nation, God would rescue the nation from defilement and from the worship of idols, giving a new heart and a new spirit to all.

The redemption Africa experiences by turning to God through Christ is not only from "wrong religion" and "wrong government," it is also from the perversions of human nature that make it possible for some to prey on others and for individuals to trample upon the humanity of others.

God is concerned for the wholeness of our *be*-ing and for our relationship to God and to other human beings. "Against thee, thee only have I sinned," said David after the scheming that resulted in Uriah's death and David's marriage to Bathsheba, Uriah's widow (Ps 51:4). God's salvation is not only open to all. It is sufficient to cover the sin of all epochs of history.

The continuity of God's action in history has to be recognized if we are not to create Yahweh in the image of our own particular age. Here I wish to refer to a crucial factor underlying the understanding of salvation in Hebrew Scriptures. The "remember you were a slave in Egypt" memory of our own salvation should make us champions of the principles of the rule of God.

> It was not because you were more in number than any other people that the Lord set his love upon you and chose you, for you were the fewest of all peoples; but it is because the Lord loves you, and is keeping the oath which he swore to your fathers, that the Lord has brought you out with his mighty hand, and redeemed you from the house of bondage, from the hand of Pharaoh king of Egypt [Dt 7:7-8].

Our salvation is absolutely undeserved. God heard our cry, saw our discomfiture, saw us distraught under our oppressors, and liberated us. This liberation is for a purpose; it is in the plan of God to make us truly human. Therefore the memory of our being a redeemed people ought to make us obey injunctions laid on us.

> You shall not pervert the justice due to the sojourner or to the fatherless, or take a widow's garment in pledge; but you shall remember that you were a slave in Egypt and the Lord your God redeemed you from there; therefore I command you to do this [Dt 24:18].

JESUS THE SAVIOR

The theme of idolatry was at the center of early Christian preaching when the early evangelists launched out into the Roman Empire. Records from the New Testament, the early Fathers, and Christian preaching in Africa show that this theme has never been ignored (see Tertullian, *De Nationes* and Athanssius, *Contra Gentes*). But to confine idolatry to the divinities of the primal religions allows us to ignore the worship of our modern idols, just as limiting the meaning of slavery to the physical sale of persons allows our modern exploitative systems to go uncriticized. Does Paul not equate greed with idolatry (Col 3:5-6)? Greed and other human failings can lead to our being alienated from God and are indeed signs of our de facto refusal to recognize the rule of God in human affairs.

No reading of the tasks that Jesus performed can fail to touch our life in Africa—as persons, nations, and as a continent. Hence the prominent use of Luke 4:18-22, the "Manifesto" of Nazareth, and of Mary's Song of Revolution, the Magnificat (Lk 1:46-55). People literally blind and in chains are added to the numbers of those blind to the demands of the kingdom of God and chained by the desire to seek their own interests as if there is no power beyond the human will. God, in sending Christ, has demonstrated the limited power of physical discomfort. He has asked us not to accept physical pain fatalistically, but with the power given us to put an end to it. In Jesus, God brings to us a style of life that puts others first, that saves others, leaving God to bring about the resurrection that will transform one's own wretchedness. Christ does not call us to use the teaching of dependence upon God to domesticate or "soften people for the kill" as some have accused Christianity of doing.[5] On the contrary, while he demands that we turn the other cheek, and pray for our persecutors as he did himself, he gives the example of refusing to stand by while *others* are being hurt, exploited, cheated, or left to die.

In the New Testament, the battle against political oppression does not loom large, but that should not blind us to its presence. Jesus did not take the dramatic approach that some of his contemporaries would have liked. He had a more radical answer: he put forward a worldview that eventually brought down the Roman Empire and that has the dynamism to break down our modern institutions that are geared toward the fulfillment of a few—if only we would obey. Instead of working toward a New Jewish Free State, he inaugurated the presence of the kingdom of God, in which *all* the people of God will be reconciled under the one rule of God. This makes him our Savior, our Yeshuah.

The Christian faith relevant to Africa demands that we associate ourselves with the work of Christ in making the angels and Dominations and Powers his subjects (Col 1:13-17), that is, subject to the kingdom of God and its values. When we say we believe in Jesus or that Jesus saves, we are referring to the one through whom God demonstrated his sovereignty over all our experiences, including death. In the New Testament account of the events, God did not save Jesus from dying, but God rescued him from death after he had been declared dead, finished, his efforts come to nothing. The centurion who stood by reversed his views when he recognized the face of God in that death. Even more significantly, Jesus' death was transformed into a new quality of life, the style of which alone will reconcile us to God. It is a life lived perpetually in the presence of God. This resurrected life is in the hands of God alone.

The good news to Africa is that people and communities have to be willing to die to all that dehumanizes on both personal and corporate levels. Those who believe that Christ lives forever, presenting us to God continually (Hb 5:7; 7:25), will venture to live a life of total dependence on God by taking what he commands seriously. Jesus saves from the insecurity that breeds distrust in God. Herein lies the particularity of Christ, whatever the culture Christ relates to the needs of the people. Outside this practical context, our theological statements and formulations have little meaning.

In the pastoral letter written to Titus (3:5) we find a doctrine on which we are called to rely. In God's compassion he saves those who are misled and enslaved by passions and luxuries, those who live in wickedness and ill will, those who hate each other and are hateful themselves, by the water of rebirth and renewal in the Holy Spirit. People and communities in Africa, having experienced this rebirth, are then to be constantly reminded, as the early Christians were, of how God rescued the nation (Israel) from Egypt and afterwards destroyed those who did not trust him (Jude 5). All nations, all Christians have to live in the knowledge of what Deuteronomy puts before Israel. A people saved by God have the kingdom of God as their priority; this is the purpose for which Jesus lived and died. Liberated from the principalities and powers of this realm we continue to work and live before God. That is salvation.

9

Covenant and Community

AGREEING TO LIVE TOGETHER

Covenants, testaments, and agreements have always been aspects of our life in community. At every turn we figuratively put our signatures to various agreements, most of them documents we have not helped to draft but to which we have to give our assent if we are to operate normally in a given community. Your signature becomes the symbol of your acceptance of the terms of participation in a particular community.

Before westernization the Akan had several ways of ratifying covenants. When they pledged a piece of land a rod was broken in two by the parties to the transaction and each kept half of it. (The Akan never sold land. The community of property arising from the community of blood made actual land sale difficult, if not impossible.) To ratify a marriage an exchange of gifts took place between the two families. Purely social agreements were never made because they could not take place without libations in which Onyame, Asaase Yaa, and the ancestors were called upon to witness and to bless.

However, there were always agreements, primarily religious in nature. They were made to the divinities and are of the nature of Hannah's vow to Yahweh (1 Sm 1:9-18). I group vows of this kind with covenants because in primal religion, when divinities become inefficient or do not fulfill their part of the bargain, they simply lose devotees. In primal societies such as those encountered in parts of the Hebrew Scriptures social agreements have a religious perspective as God is called upon to witness to them. See for instance the treaty between Jacob and Laban (Gn 31:49). The meaning of one of the three names given the border between them is *Mizpah*, "watch-post": "Let Yahweh act as watch between us when we are no longer in sight of each other." That God does watch is a firm belief among the religious people. "When you are busy making life miserable for others, God sees all parts of you, even those you try to hide, your innermost person is laid open to God." So goes an Akan proverb.

Rather than focus on types of covenants, I would like to examine the cohesive role of covenants in the human community. Vincent Mulago of Zaïre, in a paper entitled "Vital Participation, the Cohesive Principle of the Bantu Community," lists eight types of vital participation among the Bantus of Central Africa. The seventh type of participation is that of blood brothers. This union, he says, gathers into itself all the *baguma* or *bamwe* (Rwanda and Barundi words for the "one," the Unit meaning all living or dead who descend from the same eponymous ancestor, all in whom the same life, the same blood circulates in the paternal line—hence all members of the same family or clan.) Blood brothers unite their two clans because the contracting parties drink one another's blood; they have in effect a shared communion in the same life (Mulago 1968, 141–142).

Because we Africans have our roots in the same soil, drink from the same river or recognize the same divinity, a bond is created that one does not dream of breaking; it imposes a responsibility to each other that all endeavor to fulfill. Unity of life therefore is the cohesive principle in the African community. We human beings, with all created things, participate in life whose source is the One God. The enlightened world endorses Paul's quotation from the stoics that God has made the earth and all the nations of the earth of one blood. This general principle is often forgotten and has to be recalled by specific covenants such as the blood-covenant practiced between people of different clans, between members of the same cult, and sometimes even between a divinity and its devotees (Mulago 1968, 154). In most of these ceremonies, the blood is symbolized by a red liquid, just as wine represents the blood of Jesus Christ in the Christian Eucharist. The blood-covenant, as Mulago says

> can never be added to a natural union, but imitates it, and has the purpose of extending it beyond the limits of the family and the clan. It thus transcends the racial and tribal setting and opens up vast possibilities for the expansion and widening of the family [Mulago 1968, 155].

The mixing of blood, a symbol of shared life, is binding because between friends the blood-covenant actually involves mixing their lifeblood. The action underscores the sacredness and seriousness of all covenants.

Communion through shared meals takes place among people who are, or who wish to be, on peaceful and friendly terms. It is an extension of the everyday societal etiquette of the Akan, the Kikuyu, and other African peoples, and is extended not only to members of one's family or friends but even to the casual caller or the stranger. To eat from the same dish is to enter into vital relationship with the other, hence for me the pathos and tragedy of the table talk in Mark's version of the Last Supper; "It is one of the twelve, one who is dipping bread in the same dish with me" (Mk 14:20). Shared meals conclude most social and ritual events; traditional festivals often conclude with the placing of food on graves to demonstrate our continued communion with those who have gone to the other world. This highlights the daily practice of putting bits of food and drops of water on the ground before eating and makes more meaningful the more elaborate calling on the ancestors through libation. To refuse to eat is a sign of hostility; hence the polite excuse of the Akan: "My hand is in it." We Africans come to the biblical covenants from a living experience of the seriousness with which our own covenants are made.

OLD TESTAMENT COVENANTS

The Flood and the Rainbow

After the great flood, God made a covenant with Noah (Gn 8:20–22, 9:8–17) and with all living things. The rainbow was a sign, a visible and objective memorial of the promise of God. The Asante say that God is frowning when the dark rain clouds gather, and when the sun struggles through and a rainbow (Fantse, *Nyankontoñ*) appears, children shout for joy. The "Brow of God" arching clearly in the sky brings hope of a sunnier or at least a drier day.

Noah expresses his gratitude for God's past deeds by his sacrifice, but God's future, God's promise of sustained protection of creation was entirely God's own initiative and entirely one-sided. God resolved out of compassion never again to visit the earth with such devastation. But the writer sets this unconditional protection in the context of directives on what to eat and on the injunction against homicide: "I will surely require a reckoning . . . of every man's brother I will require the life of man" (Gn 9:5). This underscores the need to care for and protect others, the mutual respect for the other's being. Here the proper response to God's initiative is stipulated.

Abrahamic Covenants

A second covenant is recorded by the priestly writers in Genesis 17. This time El Shaddai, the God of the mountains, says to Abraham: "Walk before me, and be blameless. And I will make my covenant between me and you . . . " (Gn 17:1-2). The terms of the covenant as laid down by El Shaddai include the promise to be the God not only of Abraham but of the generations that will descend from him. Here the writer places the origin of the obligation to circumcise the male, but more significant is the change in names of both the man and the woman. They were from henceforth to be known by names of God's choosing, names that were a transformation of their traditional ones. Naming is important in Africa; among the Yoruba, names that connect people with one or other of the four hundred divinities are transformed to bear more directly the presence of the Supreme God: *Fabunmi/Olubunmi* (Ifa gave me/God gave me), *Awokoya/Olukoya* (the secret cult rebuffs indignity/God rebuffs indignity). We shall return to this when we examine the sacrament of baptism and the experience of African Christians.

In this covenant God dictated both sides of the obligations.

Humanly speaking the promises were ridiculous, and "Abraham fell on his face and laughed" (Gn 17:17) just as Sarah did later when God's messengers were to repeat the promise when she was within earshot (Gn 18:12). Such promises could only be made by One who is totally in charge of the universe and of human history, but without the benefit of hindsight only the knowledge of God as entirely trustworthy makes them acceptable.

Covenant at Sinai

Exodus 19:5 tells us of a covenant made not with individuals but with a whole nation, the house of Jacob, the children of Israel. The whole nation was given a law to obey and fidelity to it was imposed. When they break it they invite the anger of God and forfeit the promises attached to obedience of the law: You of all the nations shall be my very own; I will count you a kingdom of priests, a consecrated nation. The people gave their assent "All that the Lord has spoken we will do" (Ex 19:8).

Memory plays an important role here as it did in Noah's covenant: when you see a rainbow you remember God's message by flood. It is the memory of a promise. Here the people were to call to mind events in which God acted to save them—"remember what I did with the Egyptians"—as well as their own past experience of domination and exploitation—"remember you yourselves were slaves." The memory of their history was to keep them faithful to Yahweh and compassionate to the oppressed. If the God of all nations put an end to exploitation in one community we cannot expect God to condone the same exploitation elsewhere and most especially not when it comes from a people who have themselves experienced exploitation and deliverance. The covenant becomes a memorial to God's determination to rid human nature of all domineering tendencies and to establish compassion in the human community.

The Sinai covenant also indicates that having agreed to be God's people, covenanting with other nations and powers is out of the question (Dt 7:2). As a consecrated nation, a nation of priests, the Israelites record that God has directed them to an acceptable religion and that they were not to get mixed up with other religions. In a historical context, one appreciates how Israel, a small nation, had to ensure that its pastoral religion not be overcome by the exuberant agricultural religions of its neighbors. The Book of Deuteronomy shows a keen sense of this problem; it contains not only the core of the law but also several seemingly less important laws regulating cooking, for example. All these ensure that the Israelites will be distinct from the Canaanites. The Ras Shamra tablets tell us that the Canaanites cooked their veal in milk: hence the Jewish injunction against cooking "a kid in its mother's milk" (Ex 23:19 JB; see note f). Holding a common worldview is a prerequisite for perfect communion. The Hebrews operated on a strict principle of non-interaction with others for fear of losing their identity.

One element in the process of covenanting is the performance of sacrificial rites. This is of interest as it confirms our human experience of community building as involving a readiness to sacrifice. Exodus 24:4 describes how Moses built an altar to God made of twelve stones to symbolize the dedication of the twelve tribes of Israel to Yahweh. Then the people offered a holocaust to Yahweh as communion sacrifice, heard the law read, and gave their assent: "We will be obedient" (Ex 24:7). On the altar built for Yahweh, they threw half of the blood of the animals. "And Moses took the blood and threw it upon the people, and said, 'Behold the blood of the covenant which the Lord has made with you in accordance with all these words' " (v 8).

The final act as recorded in the Yahwist tradition (Ex 24:1-2, 9-12) shows the elders going up and eating and drinking in the presence of God—God and human beings in one community, a community of interests to preserve true religion and true humanity. The blood of animals shared by the two parties sealed the agreement and symbolically united them. They now share one life principle, a primal worldview that is also African. The ceremonies of the Day of Atonement (Lv 23:26-32) have several parallels in the primal religions of Africa. These similarities enabled Africans to see in Christianity a clearer expression of what they had always known. But with human beings, knowing does not necessarily mean obeying.

The Israelites' failure to live up to the covenant is dramatically presented in the Book of Judges (Jgs 2:16-19). Later Jeremiah gets to the heart of the matter: "But let him who glories glory in this, that he understands and knows me, that I am the Lord who practices steadfast love, justice, and righteousness in the earth; for in these things I delight, says the Lord" (Jer 9:24). The heart of the matter is that displaying external symbols of agreement (for example, wearing a wedding ring) does not guarantee one's faithfulness to the terms of the agreement. Therefore Yahweh will punish all those who are circumcised only in the flesh—Egypt, Judah, the sons of Ammon, Moab, the Arabs who live in the desert—all these nations and the whole house of Israel are uncircumcised at heart (Jer 9:25). Jeremiah records God's promise that the new covenant will be in the heart of each person (31:31ff.). The individual's responsibility before God is never placed second; it runs concurrently with the communal pledge to obey God. Hence the need to highlight it as seen in Ezekiel. But Ezekiel too, when he pictures renewal, sees the whole community wake up as a body, revitalized by the breath of God (Ez 36:26-27, 37). Apart from this communal and individual axis, we also are responsible for one another's well-being (Ez 34:1-9, 17-22).

Other prophets—Amos and Micah, for example—summarized God's demands in terms of social justice, love, and respect for the other, always walking in humility recognizing that we live in God's company, we are sitting at table with the Lord of the Banquet.

NEW TESTAMENT COVENANT

This leads us naturally to the New Testament covenant formally proclaimed at the Last Supper by Jesus the Christ. We read in Mark's Gospel of "my blood, the blood of the covenant" (14:24); in 1 Corinthians: "Anyone who eats and drinks without discerning the body eats and drinks judgment upon himself" (11:29). Exasperated by the behavior of the Christians at Corinth, Paul dramatizes their lack of understanding of the covenant in his description, "each one goes ahead with his own meal" (1 Cor 11:21). Some go hungry, others get drunk. If you cannot have a communal meal do not embarrass the poor. Respect their feelings; just eat in your own homes. Conspicuous consumption that ignores the needs of the poor is a problem the church in Africa has to deal with, for not only are its individual members guilty of this evil, the church itself is often guilty. The church in Africa and especially the Western churches (Roman Catholic, Anglican, Lutheran, Methodist, Baptist, Presbyterian), have a very middle-class profile. Church architecture, vestments, and interior decoration (including luxurious pipe organs) do not provide an atmosphere that is welcoming to the majority of African Christians. Yet all this is said to derive from the idea of worshipping in the beauty of holiness. Beauty has become the equivalent of a vulgar display of wealth; holiness is equated with that which is forbidding. The church becomes guilty of ostentation and conspicuous consumption, a style of life that alienates the majority of Africans who live under the burden of material poverty.

Paul sees the Christian covenant in the blood and body of Christ as uniting us with Christ (1 Cor 10:14–22). The one bread, in which we all share, forms us into one body. Paul says: "So we, though many, are one body in Christ, and individually members one of another" (Rom 12:5).

The implications of this for divided Christianity are often discussed. Not only are we not in communion with other Christians, but we are divided into rich and poor, senders and receivers, black and white. We have even created two levels of being Christian with our lay and clergy structure. All this promotes divisiveness rather than diversity.

COVENANT OLD AND NEW

Africa faces a special problem at the center of its covenant in Christ. "You cannot drink the cup of the Lord and the cup of demons" (1 Cor 10:21). On what basis do I decide between my mother's children and my brothers and sisters in Christ? When we assume that traditional covenants—because they are not made within the ambit of Christianity—are of the demon, we find ourselves in a dilemma.

Christian baptism presents us with an instance of this dilemma. Christian baptism, in that it washes away negative forces, is in perfect harmony with Africa's primal religious practices; the use of water to "wash away" is present in several traditional yearly festivals and healing processes. The idiom used by the Fantse to translate "Christian baptism" comes from the ceremony that gives new life to one who has been sick—*Bo asu*. The opposite of *Bo asu* sounds almost the same: *Gu asu*, which implies actions calculated to mess up life for another person or for one's self. It was a toss up as to whether Christian baptism was to be *asubọ* or whether the baptized were heading for self-destruction.

It did look like self-destruction since in the early days it was a sure sign that one had left one's traditional community if not physically (which also happened) at least in mentality. Baptism as an incorporation into the Body of Christ was a sacrament that could mean disloyalty to one's blood relatives. First one was given a new name. This name often superseded the one given at the naming ceremony by one's grandparents—a name that had meaning for the family and was understood by the community. By that name a person was integrated into the community and began to be a social being. Giving that name up was social death.

"Write thy new name upon my heart," says the hymnist Charles Wesley (1702–88, B 550 v.5). This "new best name of love" written on hearts comes together with the nature of God gratuitously imparted to us. The African Christian did literally receive a new name. Not only was it new, it was also strange, but pronounced to be "best." The person was marked for life as belonging to Christ. Excellent if this mark did not also bring the "stigma" of being a renegade from one's primal group. The new name Christians took with baptism meant opting out of being completely African, of belonging to a particular ethnic group; indeed, it meant opting out of the human family. Your mother and father become those who do the will of God and seek God's kingdom.

Some African Christians have sought to reconcile the two naming ceremonies by asking a Christian priest to baptize the child in the context of the traditional naming ceremony. But are the two covenants coterminus? The ethnic ceremony excludes "outsiders" as being "strangers," but not necessarily enemies or inferiors. With the belief that all human beings are the children of God, *Nnipa nyinaa yẹ Onyame Mma*, cross-group alliances are made to the benefit of all concerned. Their common interest binds them into a new community and thus widens their world. Superimposing Christian baptism on the traditional naming ceremony would be like making a blood covenant involving an individual member of the family without requiring that person to cease to have the well-being of the natural family at heart. Africans accepted Christian names as additional names and used them in church, at school, and for civil obligations of colonial structures. At home and for personal rites the name given at the traditional naming ceremony was used.[1]

African Christians became incorporated into the church and into Christ without giving up their incorporation into their human family. The situation has parallels in the early church. Christianity was launched as a universal religion based only on the acceptance of the Lordship of Christ Jesus. Its struggle was to be accepted without antagonizing the civil powers, but it clearly set out to demonstrate that its worldview superseded those of the ethnic religions with which it competed. Although emperor worship, Gnosticism, Manicheaism, and other religions were to compete vigorously with the early church, ethnic cults such as that of Diana of Ephesus were absorbed or fell into decay. The universal triumphed over the particular, but not without being expanded, modified, and redefined. Theologizing our baptism as African Christians means examining the implications of our two names, African and Christian, and the two covenants involved in the ceremonies that incorporate us into two communities.

Breaking covenants or acting contrary to their demands was the recurrent problem in the relationship between Israel and Yahweh. Liberals like Jeremiah argued that people act contrary to the covenant because they do not know or have forgotten its demands. In our day it is clear that ignorance is not the problem, but rather deliberate sin against the sovereignty of God and the oneness of the human race. The core of relationships—person to person and community to community—is examined as we examine our covenants.

What do these covenants, Christian and otherwise, aim at achieving? I believe they serve to line us up for God and humanity and against all that is of the demon. We live in a world full of demons and idols more sophisticated than any that our primal society ever knew, and we need to name them so that we may confront them. These idols have proved to be anti-life and have taken over our world. Our covenants with the demon are called a "balance of power" and they threaten to override our communion in Christ. It is the same with the idol called state security and the devil's own symbol, material wealth.

Living according to our Christian covenant demands that we say with the writer of Ephesians: "Putting away falsehood, let every one speak the truth with his neighbor, for we are members one of another" (4:25). Let us live our lives before the one God whose will is that the human community should conform to the values of the kingdom of God. When we are able to do this then we can begin to appreciate the implications of baptism and the Eucharist as sacraments building up not only our community with one another as human beings but also with God in whose image we are made and whose name is engraved on our hearts.

From the perspective of Africa, an interpretation of the Eucharist that highlights the aspect of sacrifice is one that will touch people's spirituality in such a way as to affect their lives. The victory that comes out of sharing what really costs us something is for Africans a living experience (see Oduyoye 1983). This is our path to triumph over exploitation and domination, and the way to replace charity with justice.

The link between our baptism and our frequent participation in the Eucharist is well made when we are reminded to be ready to share the baptism with which Mark begins the story of the work of Jesus, as well as the bitter cup of the crucifixion, which Jesus referred to as his baptism. The Eucharist becomes a communion, a covenant uniting us to share his mission of proclaiming and demonstrating what life under God looks like. If we wish to share the kingdom of God then we have to be ready to accept the costly sacrifice implied in our baptism. Our sacrificial life was implied by our membership in the African community and, with the coming of Christ, it has been clearly demonstrated as attainable.

The African community as part of the human community offers elements of communal yet personal caring, which the world needs and which Christ declared are ours, for even the hairs on our heads are numbered. The need to give due and appropriate place to persons and to accept what they offer the community with thankfulness can never be overemphasized. It is with this consideration in mind that I offer the next two essays: the first on the human community of women and men and the second on the Divine Godhead, the perfect example of communal being.

10

Feminism: A Precondition for a Christian Anthropology

WHAT IS FEMINISM?

I was shocked when first confronted with the French word *christianisme*. That is unfair, I thought—Christianity is not an "ism." It is far from being a partial view or an obsession; it is *the one* wholesome view of human life as lived before God. Then the warning bell rang—*wannkọ bi a wose yannko* (those who are not involved in a battle are always skeptical about the dangers of the front). I realized that my first reaction arose because of my personal involvement with the Christian worldview; there was no reason why all should share my viewpoint. From the point of view of a person of another faith, Christianity *is* an "ism," that is, a particular vision, view, or perspective that has been necessitated by other partial views, imbalances, exaggerations, and marginalizations. So it is too with feminism.

Like capitalism, socialism, communism, and sociopolitical and economic "isms" of all types, feminism implies an anthropology, a particular way of addressing itself to what it means to be human. The *logia* of each of these "isms" imply commitment to that point of view with its creed, ideology, and practices. All these aim at achieving the *agenda* that issue out of the *credenda*. Ultimately all "isms" are sectarian—such as Anglicanism, Methodism, Roman

Catholicism, and Calvinism—yet they each have something to contribute to our search for a wholesome and meaningful way of being human, and each is an elaboration of what being human is all about. Feminism is another such perspective surfacing for the Christian as part of God's project of bringing us to full humanity.

Feminism has become the shorthand for the proclamation that women's experience should become an integral part of what goes into the definition of being human. It highlights the woman's world and her worldview as she struggles side by side with the man to realize her full potential as a human being. The complex nature of feminism often goes unrecognized as people focus on the demand for linguistic changes. (That demand too needs serious consideration as we shall see later.) Feminism then emphasizes the wholeness of the community as made up of male and female beings. It seeks to express what is not so obvious, that is, that male-humanity is a partner with female-humanity, and that both expressions of humanity are needed to shape a balanced community within which each will experience a fullness of Be-ing. Feminism calls for the incorporation of the woman into the community of interpretation of what it means to be human.

But feminism is not the word of the female; it is the word of all who are conscious of the true nature of the human community as a mixture of those things, values, roles, and temperaments that we divide into feminine and masculine. It is the word of all who seek a community in which all will be enabled to attain the fullness of their being. Feminism then is part of the whole movement geared to liberating the human community from entrenched attitudes and structures that can only operate if dichotomies and hierarchies are maintained. Its reappearance in the West is a signal that even if we do not feel oppressed as a result of race or class and do not feel exploited, we may still not be living our full potential as human beings simply because we were born female or male. Feminism stands for openness, creativity, and dynamic human relationships. It has apostles among both men and women, people who believe that the question of gender has more to it than biological operations and who admit that the "female" principle and perspective have not been explored sufficiently, while the "male" has been overused to the point of stagnation, thus plunging us all into a status quo that defies analysis.

This essay illustrates some of the general statements above and outlines issues that need further research and experimentation in order to deepen our understanding of who we are as human beings. First I describe women's experience, focusing on the facts and feelings of women in Africa and of women in the Christian church. Next I examine the assumptions underlying these experiences, pointing out an ordering of society that assumes that the concept of maleness encompasses the whole of human being. I discuss the effect of language and of Christian anthropology, and attempt to understand the reason for our acceptance of the status quo. Finally I review feminism of the Christian variety in order to highlight some aspects of its liberative perspective, which will enable all to begin the march toward full humanity.

WOMEN'S EXPERIENCE: AFRICA

Women's experience of being persons primarily in relation to others—as mother or as wife—predominates in Africa. A woman's social status depends on these relationships and not on any qualities or achievements of her own. Christiana Oppong's research involving university students shows that young women of today in Africa still see themselves and are seen by their male counterparts as "somehow owned by their men who support them. They are economic attachments to men, their wage is seen as supplementary." Thus the traditional norm within which women are expected to earn an income and to provide for at least part of their own as well as their children's needs is perpetuated. So is the norm that makes housework the exclusive responsibility of women (Oppong 1976).

V. W. Turner's analysis of the "transitional rites for Ndemba girls" shows women to be pawns in sociopolitical games and alliances. The woman is the one who moves from one community to another as a result of the virilocal nature of marriage. The Nkanga marriage ritual has a "political value as an integrative mechanism." "But because at the same time it deprived other groups, such as the 'elementary family,' minimal matrilineage and often the village of a useful member, it involved loss and disturbance in a local field of kinship relations." Although the woman's personal growth strengthens the wider field of politico-kinship relations, "it confers benefits on the outside group." The loss suffered by her local group is seen as a short-term loss because "her children would come back to the lineage of their mother. . . . Thus today's loss would be tomorrow's gain" (V.W. Turner 1968, 240–268). What happens to the woman as a person is never discussed. Matriliny may give the impression of the structural dominance of women in certain parts of Africa, but (even where the marriage is not virilocal) no real power resides in the hands of the woman. As to political power, even the matrilineal, matrilocal Asante are not matriarchal. Busia points out that for political purposes the matrilineal bond is significant. But it is so only insofar as the *Ohemaa* (the queen mother) nominates the *Ohene* (the ruler). In today's Ghana and in the context of modern political power struggles, the maternal line is irrelevant. No real political power comes from one's birth by a particular woman. One may become an Asante ruler or head of the Abusua, yes, but a modern politician, no! (Busia 1951, 78).

As to the religious role of women: much as I would like to join the chorus of voices that points out women's prominence in traditional cults, experience prevents me from doing so. Traditional Africa has many cults from which women, sometimes even girls, are excluded, and some whose practices women may not even see. The Oro cult of the Yoruba and the dance of the masquerades of Kenya (boys who have just completed the seclusion and ritual that mark their transition to adulthood) are examples. Granted there are exclusive cults and rituals for women (widowhood rites, for example) but I have yet to come across one ritual that takes place in the daytime and that decrees that no males should see it. In addition the supposed ritual impurity of the menstruating woman places her outside full involvement in religious ritual for almost half her life.

Traditional sex roles in Africa operate in such a way as to make both women and men economically productive. However, women make pots that are sold cheaply; men make ritual objects and carvings that are highly regarded. Men plant yams, women have to be content with cassava. The technology that modifies men's labor is welcomed; the modernization of women's work is viewed with suspicion—African women still grind and pound the hours away. Women in Africa did not need wars to make them workers—they have always worked. The question is, what kind of work, and how has it been valued by society? What initiatives have we women been allowed? How much brain power is needed to carry on in the way I have been socialized?

The human spirit, even in Africa's tightly regulated culture, cannot be completely subjugated to community decree. Thus, in spite of all, women have broken through and insisted that the community is the poorer for putting shackles around the feet of women or of men. To cite these heroines confirms the uniqueness of their contribution; it does not exonerate the African continent from the charge of sexism.

Women's Experience: The Church

Responding to a question on the participation of women in church practices and the place of their special needs and concerns in the agenda of the church, an African woman wrote: "The women are very much concerned about the church, but the church is not so much concerned about women." This blunt statement underlies the existence of powerful Christian women's associations such as the YWCA. In lay Christian organizations the integration of women and men reflects the human community in a realistic manner, though one cannot say the same for their involvement. Church women are the acknowledged backbone of the church's finances and upkeep. Yet they rarely serve on church boards and when they do more often than not they are to represent "women's interests." A woman finally became influential in the World Council of Churches: Twila Cavert, a Presbyterian woman from the United States and a member of the YWCA. She confronted Visser't Hooft, the first General Secretary of the council, with the fact of women's contribution, and worked to have studies on the subject of women undertaken in preparation for the First Assembly of the WCC (Amsterdam, July 1948). Olive Wyon, a British theologian, had been invited as a theologian to help with the preparation of studies for the First Assembly and was asked to give "some time to the women's study" (Herzel 1981, 9; cf. Visser't Hooft 1949, 31–32).

The early history of the WCC shows the special efforts that had to be made in the provisional constitutions of Utrecht and of Amsterdam in order to insure the inclusion of the "laity—women and men." The male clericalism inherent in the structures of the church demanded this. A quota of one-third laity (women and men) was agreed upon. This goal has yet to be reached. As W. A. Visser't Hooft observed, "too few churches are willing to carry out in practice what the whole ecumenical family has so often said about the place of laity, men and women, in the life of the church" (1949, 149). After more than thirty years, women still have to make a special case to secure 12.5 percent of the seats at the Assembly of the WCC. Women have always needed advocates (such as Madeline Barot and Brigalia Bam) in the WCC Secretariat, "untiringly" reminding the WCC and its member churches of the gifts women can bring to the church and council. The council, as John R. Mott observed, reflects its member churches. The church has never tried to build a dynamic community of women and men. I never cease to be astonished at how little we have actually accomplished in community-building. The young people of Amsterdam 1948 (the WCC constitutive assembly, whose theme was "Man's Disorder and God's Design") attended as a Shadow Assembly; the women featured in the deliberations as a "concern" (WCC 1948, 29–30). This "concern" was part of Committee IV, which deliberated on "Concerns of the Churches." These included: the life and work of women in the church; the significance of the laity in the church; the Christian approach to the Jews; Christian reconstruction and inter-church aid.

Three of the recommendations that were adopted by the full commission and submitted to the Assembly read as follows:

- that an adequate supply of information about women's activities be provided through the Ecumenical Press Service (EPS) and other channels;
- that a greater number of women be chosen to serve on the commissions, major committees and the Secretariat of the WCC;
- that a commission composed of men and women be appointed, with adequate budget and executive leadership, to give further consideration . . . and to give guidance on the issues.

How contemporary! How necessary that the clericalism that developed after the early church had succeeded in putting down the Montanist movement should in our day be challenged by women! Can the church have specialists in the worship of God as the

Academy has specialists in law and astrophysics? Should women's associations continue to contribute to the maintenance of a male-dominated clergy and thereby remain supporters of the ecclesiastical status quo? (Chioma 1978).

Ancilla Kupalo, in her essay, *African Sisters Congregations: Realities of the Present Situation*, points to the tensions involved in the relationship between the mother superiors and the bishops, who expect to be consulted on the running of the congregations: "The dialogue which is the result of recognition of equality and co-responsibility is still a long way off." The process is bedeviled by the expectation of some bishops that the sisters' obedience should be "like the civil servants who always go wherever they are appointed without questioning, without consultation." Kupalo traces the relationship of superior to inferior back to "the mentality of African people, especially that of women" reinforced by the "colonial mentality of master-servant" (Kupalo 1978).

If Christian feminists have taken the stage it is to dramatize the plight of all the underprivileged and the loss to the community of their gifts and experiences. The separate development to which the church has resorted only helps to reinforce the vested interest apparent in the rest of the human community, and thus contributes to the mutilated relations and identities that are inimical to the building up of a community unashamed before God.[1] In discussions on women's involvement in the church, especially in regard to ordination to sacramental ministry, views are often expressed in such a way as to end debate—"women themselves don't want to be ordained" or "women do not like women ministers." Is it a question of what women (or for that matter men) want, or is it what God is calling us to be—"in the image of God"?

At the Amsterdam assembly Major Richard Atkinson Robinson, a Church of England delegate from the United Kingdom and Eire, asked whether any good purpose was served by embarking upon the discussion of one particular aspect of this enquiry, namely, the full ordination of women, when it was fully known that there was no hope whatever of any agreement. Others sought to sidetrack the issue by pointing out that the work of women in the church is wider than the work of women within the church. They argued that more attention should be given to the way Christian women may be equipped to more effectively make their witness in the world, since the whole moral health of the community depends on women. It was felt that, having already ordained women as deaconesses, there was nothing more to talk about. Today the reason given for not pushing the question is that we do not want to jeopardize Roman Catholic/Orthodox conversations, meaning it is better to sacrifice the community of women and men to the unity of the church (Visser't Hooft 1949, 146–152). These factors serve to becloud what may be the real reason for the reluctance of a large number of Christians to consider the ordination of women. It seems to me untheological to rule out a priori the possibility that a baptized woman may be called to the priesthood. Women do function in the church, but very few agree with the Roman Catholic woman who wrote to me:

> Personally, I am quite satisfied with the vocational opportunities available to women in the church. I feel I am doing a good job participating in the all-important work of training priests and instilling respect for women into their attitudes. It is up to women to use the opportunities afforded them.

That women are "afforded" sufficient room for ministry was already asserted at the Amsterdam assembly. The question is, what opportunities? what training? and at what price? Above all who decides the limits of these opportunities? The assumptions upon which these opinions are based have to be challenged. Here we shall look at two of them.

Two Underlying Assumptions

The first assumption is the legal one that "the greater includes the lesser." Since man is said to include woman, maleness has been made to stand for humanness, and female means either to be supportive of or to tamper with the male norm. The second assumption derives from the first. It is the linguistic assertion that male pronouns include the female and that the term *man* includes woman. Some languages, English for one, confuse the issue further by the use of "man" as both a specific and a general term. For English-using Christians this is confounded by the Hebrew word *adam* (the earth-creature), used to denote male-female or "human" and a specific human being (male) named Adam, the partner of Eve (Gn 4:25, 5:1, 3).[2]

But all this skirts the issue, for even in cultures whose languages do not have this handicap, living as a male is considered totally human as exemplified in religious ritual in which the woman's participation stops at puberty (when she "becomes" a woman) and resumes only at menopause, when she reverts to being "a man" because she no longer menstruates, that is, exhibits no sign of the ability to procreate. One would think that languages like Akan —which portrays the concept of humanity (*Nipa, Ọdasani*) as representing the wholeness of our race, which has two words for specifying the two genders (*Ọbaa, Ọbarima*, "woman," "man"), and which has two other words for "female" and "male" (*obere*, and *onini*, usually used of plants and animals)—would have stimulated the growth of a more inclusive community. Yet a study of Akan community and language discloses that its imagery is biased against the woman and puts limits on the man. The popular naming of a truck "Fear Woman" is interesting when compared with the expression *ọbarima nsuro wuo*, "a man does not fear death."

In every society role assignment based on gender stereotypes has a hemming-in effect on both women and men. The man who is banned from the kitchen comes to believe that a man would have to reach the limits of despair to cook for himself. In a society that does not have restaurants and yet by tradition excludes menstruating wives from touching food, the man solves his problem by resorting to polygyny. Yet this same society says "a man with two wives is a double-tongued one." There is a dynamic relationship between our myths and imagery and what we actually do. It is common knowledge, for instance, that Western education for girls lagged behind that for boys because of the unprofitability of an educated daughter to her parents. She will get married and the benefits that come from the investment will accrue to her husband. That the education will be of benefit to *her as a person* is not considered because only the biological aspect of her Be-ing is important.

The man/woman typologies we have around us have conditioned us to the extent that we are embarrassed by any suggestion that things could be different. It is therefore to be expected that feminist protest about language should be ridiculed by some men and should embarrass many women. Even those who feel modifications are overdue raise the issue in an apologetic manner. In theological circles the question of language use has called into inquiry the things we say about God. If God is spirit, why should we feel alienated by the application of both male and female imagery?—we have to speak anthropomorphically. Are we at home using male terms in relation to God because we see the male as the superior created being, or is there some deeper reason/revelation at work?

Why is "chairman" more acceptable than "chairperson"? The WCC chose the term "moderator," but it became "madame moderator" when the moderator was a woman and simply "moderator" when the moderator was a man. Is this indicative of inertia, or does it signify a deep-seated reluctance to acknowledge that the business of chairing a meeting can be undertaken equally well by a woman as by a man?

In the present state of man/woman relationships, our culture-bound typologies condition not only the individual but also the whole community to believe that labels are decreed by God. Are they? The authority of tradition can only be binding when, upon examination and testing, it is found to be the best we can have at the moment. Feminists (and others who feel their oppression) do not believe that the present ordering of human relations furthers our ultimate good. Sexist criteria cripple rather than enable, and their tendency to subsume the woman under the man suggests that we believe the needs of the male are more important than those of the whole community. Yet we can all say that neither the male nor the female is greater than the community, for the community transcends the joint existence and contribution of the women and men who compose it. The interaction of the composite parts is of utmost importance and the terms of interaction ought to be evolved by both partners. We need to examine the extent to which the religious myths and language we employ mirror existing social relationships and how these relationships in turn show us how "true" those sayings are (Oduyoye, *Socialization*).

The language of Christianity needs to be reexamined as much as do the languages of other religions.

CHRISTIAN ANTHROPOLOGY REVISITED

The whole human community and each of its component parts—family, industry, church—are affected by the culture-bound view of humanity that puts limits on creativity. One of the themes that has come in for reexamination is the *Imago Dei*. The teachers of the early church had definite opinions on the liberation of the human spirit and its meaning for man-woman relationships. The first creation narrative was underplayed in the biblical history of salvation and became useful when Christianity had to deal with the Greek philosophical idea of the *logoi spermaticoi*. Athanasius used it in his *De Incarnatione*: Christ, the Image of God, restores the tarnished image of God in us.

In trying to deal with the concept of the tarnished image the narratives of Genesis 2 and 3 are called into play. This concept also leads to speculation and arguments about the biblical material. Does it suggest that the woman is not made in the image of God in the same way that the man is? God, who transcends gender, is yet "imaged" in male terms, and the road is clear for the female to be seen as created in the image of the male and not directly of God. A few illustrations from the early Church Fathers may be apposite here, although only an intensive study of their writings will be of real value in this search for the meaning of being human. There is no doubt that the image we have of ourselves as Christian women and men and of our community and the language we use in speaking of ourselves have been shaped by these thinkers.

Commentaries on the creation narratives, moral exhortations and Christian salvation history afforded the Fathers the opportunity to comment on the humanity of the woman. Tertullian's moral exhortation *On Women's Dress* gives us one example:

> The judgement of God upon your sex endures even today; and with it inevitably endures your position of criminal at the bar of justice. . . . You are she who persuaded him whom the Devil was not strong enough to attack. So easily did you shatter the image of God in man. Because of your reward which is death, even the Son of God had to die [ed. Anne Fremantle, *A Treasury of Early Christianity*, Viking Press, N.Y.: 1953].

Tertullian is really telling women to dress modestly so as not to be stumbling blocks to men. It is a well-known Western attitude that the community's sexual morality depends on the "purity" of women. This belief is also found in other religions and cultures. What reality lies behind this demand? In Christian thinking sexuality has been singled out as the root of human troubles. Gregory of Nyssa, in his Homilies on Genesis 1:26 and his treatise *On the Making of Man*, argues that "while not evil in itself, it was provided by God for the procreation of the race when he foresaw that man would fall away from his original angelic nature."

Women's sexuality is deemed to be a necessary evil. Should we allow this assessment to go unexamined? Gregory also says that "the likeness implied by the 'image' comprehends all the divine attributes" (Baillie, et al. 1953, 239). Athanasius takes a different approach and locates our likeness mainly in our being rational beings. In *De Incarnatione* he writes on the rationality of the human being:

> . . . giving them a portion even of the power of his own Word; so that having as it were a kind of reflection of the Word, and by being made rational, they might be able to abide ever blessed, living the true life which belongs to the saints in paradise [Baillie, et al. 1953, 276].

Here we note a play on the words *logos* and *logikos*. But the question remains: in what does being made in "the image and likeness of God" consist? If sexuality is a necessary evil why should it curtail the involvement of the woman with what is sacred and not curtail the man's involvement? Can we continue to affirm Genesis 1:26 and then carry on as if the image of God meant nothing when applied to the woman? The tangle of questions raised by culture, Christian tradition, and church practices leaves one with no choice but to call the rationality of the conscious beings that we are into play.

Undoing the Tangle

In untangling the web of oppression one begins to appreciate what happens to a ball of cotton when a kitten plays with it. There is one thread at the center of the ball of our distorted likeness of God. This one thread is our refusal to measure up to the image of God, our firm refusal to allow others the chance to reveal the image. At the center of the intricate web of human concerns is our distortion of our God-likeness.

Feminists say that, whereas there are many ways of approaching the interconnections of oppressive structures, one necessary dimension is to recognize that women do feel thwarted by existing arrangements. Finding a way to release the oppressed must include taking women's experience of structures seriously. The tendency is to pass over as a joke what women say about the constraints they feel in their lives. To undo the tangle we must take account of women's experience. In this respect assumptions concerning sexuality are being called into question. Can we say with André Dumas, professor of theology of the Faculty of Protestant Theology in Paris, that "sexuality is only the physical expression of what is happening in the depths of the personality" when the "personality" we exhibit has been molded by a sexist community? (Herzel 170–173).

Henrietta Visser't Hooft's question on 1 Cor 11:5–11 to Karl Barth instigated some interesting correspondence between the two. She wrote: "What does Paul mean when he says 'man was not created for woman's sake, but woman for the sake of man'?" Barth's response was:

Paul did not write all that in order to reach and canonize a certain concept of the relation between man and woman; he took that relationship (which he considers the right one) to illustrate the relation between God and man, as it should exist in the Christian community. . . . Admittedly the question still remains, why Paul used this concept of male superiority to describe God's superiority to human beings. . . . Not only Paul, but the whole Bible, assumes that the man-woman relationship on earth and in time is not matriarchy but patriarchy [Herzel 1981, 171].

The feminist question is, does it have to be one or the other? Henrietta Visser't Hooft asked whether the man-woman relation should not be conceived along the lines of mutual interest, trust, and responsibility. To this Barth responded:

> I am afraid Paul could *not* have expressed what he wanted to say in terms of your concept of the man-woman relationship. For between God and human beings there can be no "mutual interest," there can only be superiority!

Perhaps we should all follow Barth's advice and concentrate our thinking on the points he makes. The Pauline analogy is not beyond criticism, for if there is no mutual interest between women and men, then where shall we begin to build our human community? Is mutuality between man and woman out of the question? What is the significance of a woman's life if male superiority is used to describe divine superiority and she is then shown her obligation to accept not only God's but also that of the male?

Both women and men must reexamine Christian tradition and confront those aspects that justify the domestication of women. We must reread those teachers who are able to say with Gregory Nazianzen: "One same Creator for man and woman. For both the same clay, the same image, the same law, the same death, the same resurrection" (Behr-Sigel n.d.).

The Acceptance of Brokenness

"Separate development" and "job reservation," decried in other contexts, are the norm in the broken community of men and women. In some churches our brokenness even shows itself in the seating during worship. The aspirations a Christian woman should have were prescribed at a consultation held in Beirut in 1980. The mission of the twentieth-century woman was

> to forget herself so that she would melt like a candle to bring light to those who are around her. . . . Confront waves with firmness and steadfastness. . . . She has to be the rock on which waves of hardships break, yet hold out. . . . Should she collapse, the whole structure of her family would collapse as well [Middle East Council 1980, 22–26].

Women were then called upon to abandon the consumer mentality that would send them to work outside the home and were advised to "go back to nature" and to "housekeeping." This speaker said that by so doing women would symbolize the Motherhood of God. According to this theory it is the absence of woman that is felt; her presence in the home is taken for granted. The man's absence from home and family is taken for granted. The woman who works outside the home does so *in extremis*. However, Asante market women interviewed on this view of woman said they had to struggle hard to educate their children and to supply their children's needs because their men were irresponsible. Asante women, who for generations have owned property and have contributed to the economy, still believe that when they do these things they are really doing men's work. That they are simply fulfilling a share of a mutual responsibility is not part of their worldview. The woman is to bear children and keep house; anything she undertakes beyond the home puts her in the double-taxation syndrome. This may be illustrated in different aspects of life.

The feelings of women around these issues are ridiculed. Thus the human personality is fractured into objective and subjective, rational and emotional, and the head is given prominence over the heart. We have thus succeeded in destroying the mutuality that must exist in order to evolve an integrated community enriching to all. To work toward such a community requires that we face our brokenness in a realistic manner, but this is resisted by many, both women and men.

We accept this brokenness because we have a misconception of the human core of our relationships. A recent World Council of Churches study on the "Community of Women and Men in the Church" has unveiled much of what one can call by no other name than male-domination. It has revealed how many lives are lived according to unexamined norms, according to unquestioned assumptions and myths. These reinforce the brokenness that we all live. If no one is hurt, the corporate acceptance of what is, could continue; but if some in the community feel and express a hurt, then the corporate life can only be described as sick. It will remain an ailing body until we each develop a sensitivity toward the full humanity of the other.

A Liberating Perspective

The responsibility for healing our brokenness falls on men and women alike. The female perspective is a crucial dimension since it has not been given a chance to become integrated into the existing basis of our relationships. The Be-ing of the woman is reduced to nothingness because she is habitually ignored. Woman's self-definition has lacked authenticity and so carried no authority because woman is not an "agent." The feminists call us to explore anew our human Be-ing and to affirm each one's mode of being human. Because man and woman are created in the same image does not mean that we are not distinctive beings with varying predilections.

In order to begin the experiment of fully human living, whatever gender we are, we are called to refuse to be what others require us to be, instruments against our own convictions, people who acquiesce to their own marginalization. Positively put, we are called to struggle for the transformation of relationships. We have to live the life of the future even as we seek to bring it into existence by our insistence on personal accountability, participation, and on the importance of becoming authentic reflectors of the Image of God. In this way we may hope to build a human community whose obligations arise from within ourselves rather than from outside pressure. This view challenges the traditional view of authority. It is a part of the liberation process that will surely encompass all persons.

TOWARD WHAT WE ARE

What then is the feminist contribution to anthropology—what it means to be human in the community of women and men? First we must admit the feminine experience as a legitimate part of the data for theological reflection or we will continue to live in our brokenness. But whether or not our anthropology is based on a theology, the woman's experience must be taken into account. In this section I take as my point of reference only what Christianity says God is calling women and men to become.

Christian feminists have emphasized some of the biblical typologies that place women and men equally before God in order to balance our one-sided reading of the Scriptures. Women and men are depicted by Scripture as being equally the objects of God's love. They experience God's love to the extent that their personal inclinations allow. The variety of gifts described in Acts had no gender limitations; neither does the list described by Paul. The will of God in the matter of who does what is for me declared clearly by what women—freed from cultural taboos, though constrained by circumstances or tradition—have been able to contribute to the human community. Being "a little lower than the gods" applies equally to both men and women, just as sin knows no gender boundaries. The myths that seek to blame the woman do not exonerate the man; both are endowed with the ability to respond to God and baptismal grace knows no sexist boundaries.

A key issue in the search for authentic humanity is the role and source of authority. In what measure or on what basis do we allow the demands of authority, continuity, and stability to shape our potential of turning to good or evil? Where or what is the ultimate source of authority for the human community and how do we receive this authority? Christians are called to examine anew the meaning of the Bible. Liberation theology calls for this examination as our traditional apologetics on behalf of biblical authority becomes less and less convincing. The idea of authority itself needs reexamination.

Feminist theologians have been critical of the dualistic and hierarchical modes of conceiving and organizing the human community and of its various levels of interaction. They have emphasized the necessity of giving mutuality and partnership a chance, not just in man-woman relationships but in all human enterprises. The call for relational language about God is to be seen in this light.

If male language about God has resulted in our imagining God in male terms and if we feel uncomfortable about female language where God is concerned, then we have to try a third way. Relational language about God may provide us with integrated models of community. God is creator, and being like God, we create. We too are active beings cooperating with God in the business of creation. The Christian proclamation that God is not a nomad but rather a center of relations in which Father, Son, and Holy Spirit act and interact without subsuming or subordinating any of the Persons and yet act as One toward the world—may provide us with a model of the integrity of persons within community and their interrelatedness. An examination of what the early church was trying to say in the doctrine of the Trinity may yield models for building the human community—not on a hierarchy of beings but on the diversity of gifts that operate in an integrative manner.

Our baptism into Christ compels us to see ourselves as the beginning of a new humanity modelled after Christ. Just as Galatians 3:27–28 has been evoked on behalf of the abolition of slavery and racism, so the feminist in these latter days evokes it to show that sexism is incompatible with our being in Christ. We are baptized into Christ as persons, irrespective of our social status, so that just as the humanity of the male is taken into the Christ so is the humanity of the female. There is no sexual distinction in the Trinity, but qualities labelled feminine and masculine are all manifested in Christ Jesus who is the image par excellence of God.

A Christian contribution to the *isms* that seek to shape the meaning of life needs the experience of women, since above all it calls for a return to God-intended relationships that we have lost through our dichotomizing sexuality and making its biological manifestations and implications the foundation of our human relations. Woman's experience of the human community unearths many shortcomings arising from sexism's tendency to shape the extent of our being as creative, caring creatures, who, after the image of God, conquer chaos to bring forth good out of a nebulous existence. No one can claim to be in the image of God who is insensitive to the cry of the afflicted, who invests in structures of domination, or supports them because of vested interests.

We cannot be happy and unashamed in each other's company if we are hiding behind our gender to shirk responsibility. As baptized people, our suffering is salvific when taken on voluntarily and our sharing of the gifts of others gives us the ability to thank God who made us male and female. Happy and responsible in my being human and female, I shall be able to live a life of doxology in the human community, glorifying God for the gifts I receive in others and for the possibility I have of giving myself freely for the well-being of the community while remaining responsible and responsive to God. It is only thus that I can say I am fully human. When we are all willing to see the humanity of the other, then we can begin the task of understanding a Christian anthropology.

11

Trinity and Community

Today's search for meaningful theological ways in which to express the Christian faith takes one of two forms: dogmatics or problematics. Dogmatic theologians maintain the classical statements of the faith as embodied in the Chalcedonian definition. Some theologians construe the task as one of reformulating dogma in order to make it comprehensible, for both the structure and the content are divinely revealed and therefore permanently valid; others question the fundamentals of those classical statements, and ask whether the formulas handed down to us really fit the seminal experience that generated them. Thus, in dogmatics, contemporary theologians are reexamining the basic tenets of Christianity.

The other type of theology on the contemporary scene is problematics. Problematics, John Hick says,

> takes place at the interfaces between the tradition and the world—both the secular world and the wider religious world—and is concerned to create new theology in the light of new situations [Hick 1980, 1].

The world, of course, does not ignore traditions; neither is tradition used only as part of an academic intellectual gymnastics. If it were, the exercise would not be theology, for theology is no less than our attempt to give reasoned expression to our belief in God. We do that in this body and in this world, although it is related to our ultimate concern.

138

CONTEMPORARY THEOLOGY

Contemporary Christian theology addresses itself to both dogmatics and problematics. In recent times dogmatics has become well known through several publications such as J. A. T. Robinson's *Honest to God* and John Hick's *The Myth of the Incarnate God*; problematics has been highlighted in James Cone's *God of the Oppressed*, Gustavo Gutiérrez's *A Theology of Liberation*, and Basil Moore's *Black Theology: A South African Voice*. Both dogmatics and problematics have raised theological issues that demand further elaboration in forms that take account of people's histories —communal and individual.

In Africa, the issues of salvation and liberation; creation, ecology and stewardship; racism and the unity of humankind are all being explored. All over the world questions of the uniqueness of Jesus Christ in world history are being raised in new and fascinating ways, and interest in the personhood of the woman raises questions not only of beliefs and practices but also of the relationship between them. Dogmatic or problematic, Christian theology always applies itself to the basic beliefs of Christianity.

Concern for the indigenization of Christianity in Africa has brought about the adaptation of African ritual and forms but not of restatement of the faith. The doctrine about God's nature that declares a sharing of enterprise as well as of glory becomes burdensome and imprecise when translated into human terms and applied to human relationships. Nevertheless, this is precisely the point at which the doctrine must be studied, understood, and lived. The divine economy (*oikonomia*, the way God operates) ought to be approximated in human relations.

LIVING OUT THE TRINITARIAN LIFE

From the gospels we clearly see that Jesus came with a unique way of looking at the world. He spoke and lived a life that declared that the only reality in this world is God. He taught that all our attempts at securing ourselves, our self-concern (or is it selfishness?) are basically atheistic. Bultmann would call this the original sin (Soelle 1969, 60). Jesus insisted that the only way to secure true life was to lose ourselves. This was a completely new perspective on human life, and a radical departure from the recommendation of unredeemed human nature. It envisaged a new creation. For this to happen the world needed a movement of healing and restoration. Christianity claims to be such a movement; it claims to embody "the faith of Jesus" (Vidler 1963, 106).

It is from this stand that I view the ethical function of the Trinity. Living a life of faith in God demands a radical reassessment of salvation. This includes first and foremost a reconception of the importance of self and of our well-being as individuals. A life of faith in God demands participation at all levels for all. This style of life calls for cooperation, not determined attempts to succeed on one's own. The truth of what Jesus has said about the world and about God is not something you can expect others to accept simply because you have taught them. They will only come to know as they begin to walk along the Way. Our relation to truth cannot be theoretical. The question then is this: Can a group of people function in such a way that they will not be submerged as individuals, but there will exist such a concerted atmosphere that one can live for all and all for one? We see in the Godhead how "several centers of consciousness are integrated with and related to one another" (Brown 1969, 60). We find the Persons in constant and perfect mutual relationship and we are reminded of the need for properly adjusted relationships in our human families, institutions, and nations. Hodgson asks us to see the doctrine of the Trinity as "a distinction of Persons with a closeness of unity characteristic of modes of existence" (Hodgson 1954, 45). Similarly, both the unity and the diversity in a community will be seen as important.

Traditionally the doctrine of the Trinity was a response to this problem of the early Christians: they could not "reduce" all of God to the human incarnation and yet they were convinced of the lordship of the risen Christ. Does this speak to our political problem of the place of the individual relative to the community? The community of three in the one Godhead is certainly more than Father plus Son plus Spirit; each Person is distinct and yet the community is a reality because of the way in which it functions. Saint Basil's response to the Augustinian formula *opera trinitatis ad extra sunt indivisa* (originally put forward by the Cappadocian

Fathers) was: "It is the names that distinguish them, not the activities, for in that, they are perfectly indistinguishable."[1] I observed this in my relationship with my parents, as did other children; we nicknamed the syndrome "the echo" in recognition of the harmony of their response to us.

In the Son, the Trinity shared and continues to share in the suffering and evil of this world, just as in the Spirit the Godhead continues to be our constant guide into all truth. One could say that it is only in community that our humanity means anything. Experiencing Jesus was for the disciples an experience of God's self-revelation, and the Spirit that guided their lives they described as the Spirit of God. What does this say to life in our human community?

A hint of a political theory is contained in Barkway's words on the practical value of the doctrine of the Trinity:

> The manifoldness of the divine nature contains the treasure and truth after which polytheism was grasping in its array of many gods. . . . Similarly . . . the opposite truths [were] expressed by deism, with its emphasis on the absolute transcendence of God, and pantheism, with its insistence on his all-pervasive presence [Barkway 1957, 75].

The constitutions of federal governments are illustrative of our human search for a just balance of the one and the many. Polytheism is a similar example of the search for unity in diversity. When communities model themselves on polytheistic structures, emphasis is apt to be placed on the units that make up the community rather than on the whole. Decisions and lifestyle generally will be dictated by individuals' powers, rights, and needs. This orientation toward the component parts of a community fragments community solidarity and is likely to lead to anarchy since each unit becomes more or less a separate entity. Structures and systems that then try to have authority over the whole are bound to create rancor when they operate at cross-purposes with the aspirations of the units of which the whole is composed. We thus have examples of countries that run themselves, so to speak, countries in which national politics seems to play a minimal role and business runs the show. Such systems, impersonal and bureaucratic, may result in a uniformity that would make human life dull and meaningless. The trinitarian model is full of vitality, and its energy is generated by love, participation, and sharing. It is a model that gives unique meaning to our being created in the image of God.

At the meeting of the Commission on Faith and Order (Bangalore, 1978), Metropolitan Mar Osthathios commenting on the first draft of the commission's message said:

> The unity of humanity is to be modeled on trinitarian unity. . . . Ultimately all differences and separations between human beings have to be dissolved in a mutual *perichoresis* [embracing, penetrating, not merely sharing] where "thine and mine" are not different in case of property, purpose and will but different only in different personal and group identities with full openness to and penetration of each other. . . . The mystery of the unity of humanity in Christ, patterned on the mystery of the triune unity in the Godhead, has high significance for our social goals also. . . . Ultimately, parochialism, insularity, division, separation, class, ethnic conflict, political and economic injustice, exploitation and oppression have to be judged by this criterion [WCC 1978, 1–11].

The struggle to hammer out sociopolitical ideologies capable of inspiring our life together has been bedeviled with all sorts of *isms*. The statement Mar Osthathios made is an attempt to spell out the meaning and practice of the *sensus communis* as understood (if not fully practiced) in traditional Africa.

The oldest form of human *isms*, sexism, was also examined at Bangalore. German theologian Jan Milic Lochman, reporting on a preparatory meeting, said:

> The Unity-in-diversity of the Holy Trinity points to true community. God is One and Unbroken, yet has relationships among the three persons. God relates inwardly and outwardly. . . . Likewise human communities have unity, yet they must encompass diversity [WCC 1978, 1–11].

Lochman was reporting on "Discipline of Communion in a Divided World of Women and Men." Christian theology has not presented the Trinity simply as a more adequate metaphysical symbol of deity but has attempted to demonstrate the Trinity's value as a model for human relationships. The relevance of the doctrine for contemporary theology then becomes apparent. But Christian doctrines have relevance not only on the horizontal plane. We therefore have to examine our vertical relationship to the deity in the light of these doctrines.

THE TRINITY AND THE SACRAMENTS

Our baptism into the name of the Trinity means that we should stand not for monarchies and hierarchies but rather for participation.[2] In God's economy we find a sharing of power and of responsibility. The result of action is attributed to all three Persons. The unity that exists in the Trinity does not have simple analogies in creation; both the threeness and the oneness are different from anything we know in finite society. Nevertheless the principles of analogy and of symbolic language allow us to hope that human society will at least try to get rid of the kind of distinctions that kill unity.

Our baptism into the name of the Trinity also means that we share Jesus' acceptance of solidarity with sinners that led him on the path of self-giving, not just on behalf of the baptized, but on behalf of the whole world. Through baptism we take part in the trinitarian economy toward the salvation of the whole world.

In the Eucharist we give thanks to the Blessed Trinity for creating, redeeming, sanctifying, and for all the other benedictions that creation receives at the hands of the Three-in-One. We give praise on behalf of the whole world, which God has reconciled to Godself. In the *anamnetic*, the "remembering," aspect of the sacrament we focus specifically on God the Son; in the *epiklesis,* the "invocation," we pray to the Holy Spirit. In the Eucharist we demonstrate our faith in the unity and diversity that is God. In this act of worship we also find communion as Christians and a representation of the goal of salvation, namely the fulfillment of the kingdom. If this is so, then the Eucharist should mean that the world is the church's business. Should it not also mean that both the unity and the diversity that is the church are God-given? Should we not emphasize diversity rather than division, wholeness rather than uniformity? The ability to sing the Doxology depends upon our saying Yes to diversity.

THE ONENESS OF THE CHURCH

In recent times both the World Council of Churches and the Vatican have reiterated what the Eastern Orthodox Churches have always maintained—that the ground and the goal of the church is the Blessed Trinity (see Williams 1966, 22–42; cf. WCC 1960, 12–44). One can, then, go to the doctrine of the Trinity to see if it can enable us to free ourselves of misconceptions about the unity of the church. The Cappadocians, in their attempt to incorporate the ideas of the full substantial divinity of the Son and the Spirit into the old pattern of monotheism, modified the idea of unity. As Platonists they insisted that the unity of divine activity is evidence against any division of the divine *ousia*. The church accepted this. But was the church ready to apply this differentiated unity of God to itself? Only in recent times has the church begun to think in terms of organic unity and visible unity. Previously the goal seems to have been the organizational unity of the church, not only locally but also universally.

Take the baptismal controversy that followed the Decian persecution as an example. Cyprian would not accept Novatianist baptism because he believed that the church of which he was head was the only church. He appealed to Rome in a bid to make his stand the Catholic policy, but Stephen of Rome was of a different opinion. Stephen recognized a differentiated unity as far as validity of sacraments was concerned. Thus he gave us the principle behind the formulation that the Christian who disagrees with you is not necessarily a heathen. Later bishops of Rome were not so liberal. Augustine too recognized Donatist baptism and ordination. On this account should not the Cyprianic concept of the unity of the church be reinterpreted?

If Augustine could tell the Donatists that the holiness of the church is eschatological, why did he refuse to say that the true unity of the church is also eschatological? Why did he take his stand with Cyprian and define empirical unity as one organization? Should the organic unity of the Trinity which we confess (although we do not fully understand it) not make us tolerant of the idea of organic unity of the church? Should our confession of the unity of activity of the Trinity toward the world steer the church toward unity of action on behalf of the world, we shall be working towards the visible unity of the church.

The church, we all agree, "is the one body of Christ (mystically constituted) in which members have union and are united by the sacraments [baptism and eucharist]" (O'Neill, 1966, 30–42). Of course diversity is evident—diversity of members, offices, mode of worship, organization. Is it too much to claim that all this is geared toward a common purpose by the Spirit and in charity?

CONCLUSION

It would be easier to write off the doctrine of the Trinity as nonsense, a mystery, a metaphysical puzzle, even as blasphemy than to attempt to see what I think is being revealed through this expression of faith. To confess the reality on which the doctrine is based is to discover a valid basis on which we can live truly human lives. We are clearly not ready for this—not only as individuals, but also as families, institutions, nations, and churches. Not even the primitive church, which struggled to formulate the doctrine, was ready for its implications. All our human organizations are convicted by the standards of the trinitarian community.

If the church lives out the implications of the Trinity, Christians will have no problem in claiming that the doctrine is relevant even though inexplicable. The doctrine will be seen as important for understanding reconciliation and redemption and for the fulfillment of our humanity after the shape of the Godhead. I am not saying that the doctrine of the Trinity is indispensable, although some have died for it. What I am saying is that "now we see through a glass darkly" and that the symbols of our faith should be allowed to inform our life together in God's world as God's people.

Postscript

I offer in these essays an open-ended account of what my reflections on Christianity in Africa lead me to say about Christian faith. Growing up in the church, listening to the church through preaching, songs, prayers, and the decisions of ecclesial bodies, being part of the African world as it goes through a continuous experience of change—one cannot describe in terms of immovable givens what exactly it is one knows. Through all these God is experienced as working to become better known. The historical realities I live and the church's involvement in them are for me a witness to what God is doing in and with the world. To seek a prophetic and liberative role for Christian theology in this context means also to analyze what the church has been and is, as well as what Africa has been and is.

Today there is no need for an apologia on contextualization of theology. It is generally accepted that theology cannot but be contextual. In Africa, adaptation as a processing of theological thought forms is not new; it is flourishing in the charismatic Africa churches and is becoming more precise for the formal construction of theology that will be meaningful.

Some Africans do not feel able to relate to this search for meaning by way of Africa's total experience because they see the categories in which Western Christian theology has been set as unchangeable and adequate for all times and places. I have given space to their views because they represent a view of Christianity in Africa that is not likely to go away but rather has the potential to become even more influential. For my own part, I see the pastoral concerns that gave rise to the early theologies of indigenization and their liturgical and organizational manifestations as issues with which the church in Africa continues to grapple. These concerns are becoming more complex as the technology and the politico-economic interdependence of the world produce more and more complex ethical problems for people in Africa. My concern is with the church and with the question of how Christianity can play a transforming role in Africa and avoid becoming a source of ideologies that acquiesce to injustice and de-personalization. The church as an institution needs members who will make it relevant, not only to what they are but also to what they will become.

African theologians have moved from debates about what African theology is, or is not, and from discussions of what it might become. The period of advising others on what to do in order to give birth to an authentic and relevant African theology is moving to one of expressions of the faith by Africans who have had formal theological education with all the scientific discipline that it involves. These do not render otiose the earlier building blocks, which may provide future generations with ideas that will generate other routes to the explication of Christian faith in Africa. I affirm people's freedom to approach issues from their best insights. African theology will comprehend all of Africa and of Christianity and so cannot help but be variegated. I have in these essays attempted to see the gospel as coming into dynamic relationship with people's spirituality as well as with their socioeconomic and cultural realities. What I have written comes out of my reflections on Christianity in the light of my experiences as an African Christian and a church woman.

Africa belongs to the world of the powerless and the dispossessed. As a woman who feels the weight of sexism I cannot but go again and again to the stories of the exodus, the exile, and to other biblical motifs in which "the least" are recognized and affirmed, are saved or held up as beloved of God or at least are empowered to grow at the fundaments of the structures of injustice until these fundaments cave in on themselves. These narratives have been for me the bearers of good news.

Therefore in spite of the entrenched patriarchal and ethnocentric presuppositions of the Bible, it is a book I cannot dispense with and indeed may not since I remain in the Christian community and that community means more to me than my personal hurts. For the same reason I cannot be anything else but African. And so, bringing my whole be-ing and life experience to bear upon what I hear of

God through Christ, I appropriate for myself a theory of knowledge that does not permit me to see truth as a given that I have to accept or reject. Rather I see myself, in community with others and in the enabling power of the Holy Spirit, called to participate in growing into a fuller understanding of what God is about. Neither the Bible nor the African corpus of sociocultural history can be treated as fossilized touchstones. Critical apparatus exist for their use, and theologians are making others aware of this factor.

In my reflections I have not ruled out in an a priori fashion the possibility of coming to know Christ more fully, of comprehending God's future better, and of listening for what the Spirit is saying to the churches and to the African world. For this reason in these reflections I seek understanding not only from the Bible and the Christian tradition but also from what some may deem unlikely sources. When I read theological theory my pragmatic approach to life is at its keenest where prescriptions are decreed. I never cease to ask myself who is benefiting from a particular stance? Theology bears the marks of ideology.

In the Akan worldview that operates in the dark mysterious center of my being there sits a sense of my being mystically incorporated into an ever expanding principle of human be-ing. Hence my attraction to the dialectics of the themes of community and selfhood. Liberation/freedom/salvation from such a stance cannot be conceived as being experienced at the expense of "the other." As I reflect on this, other thoughts are generated, which have only been hinted at in these essays. Here indeed is a theology en route.

As we Africans re-read the Bible and books on Western missionary theology, we unmask their ideological components, but we draw toward the ecumenical truths they embody and are thereby freed to move to re-interpretation and re-statement and to uncover aspects of the truth that may have remained concealed to the Western mind.

We heard about sin and evil in humanity and in African culture; now we know and can name the structures of injustice. The embodiments of evil and sin take on broader and deeper meaning. We do not simply name, we seek empowerment from the gospel to dismantle what is demonic in society and to exorcise the demons that turn persons into oppressors. We heard the mission theology of the salvation of individual souls; now we know that salvation cannot but be in a familial context and encompasses the whole person as an integrated being.

We heard about being created in God's image and as such being moral agents, a little lower than the gods, knowing good and evil and able freely to respond to God. Now we know that to be fully human we have to have the freedom to respond, to initiate, and to participate. We have to have the freedom to be able to obey God rather than human beings. We heard "you shall have no other gods," and now we know that any response made because of the principalities and powers of this world rather than because of a faith-in-God stance is idolatry. We heard of the dangers of attempting to find out whether God indeed has witnesses in all human cultures, and we felt the dismissal of African culture. Now we know we are not alone in our search, and we attempt to respond to the Christ who confronts us in the Bible, who comes to us as African women and men, black and poor people of the South who are prone to the manipulations of the rich North. Knowing ourselves, having a sense of history, believing in the future and the transformation brought about by the cooperation of the divine and the human in Jesus the Christ, we are (I am) freed to take part in the building up of theologies that will contribute to the transformation needed in the church and in society.

Notes

INTRODUCTION

1. Representatives of twenty-nine countries participated in the Bandung Conference (1955). Most of them came from countries newly liberated from colonial rule or from countries determined to stay out of the East-West politico-economic debate of the Cold War. Members of the Ecumenical Association of Third World Theologians (EATWOT) came from a wider geographical area.

2. See Baëta 1981. Baëta, a Ghanaian, studied under Karl Barth and was for many years head of the Department for the Study of Religion, University of Ghana, Accra.

3. See J. A. T. Robinson's *Honest to God* (1963) and John Hick's *The Myth of God Incarnate* (1977). Both of these books created lively debate. See also Dorothee Soelle's *Political Theology* (1974) and Letty M. Russell's *The Liberating Word* (1976).

4. The lectures were later published as a book (see Becken 1973) and then reissued with some additions (see Moore 1973).

5. Papers from the Fifth International Conference of EATWOT have been published in book form (see Fabella and Torres 1983). Papers from another pertinent meeting, the Asian Theological Conference (Sri Lanka, 1979), have also been published (see Fabella 1980).

1. EARLY CHRISTIAN THEOLOGY IN AFRICA

1. I use the term "Nile Basin" to designate the Christianized areas of Egypt, Ethiopia, and Nubia as found in the early and medieval periods. Ecclesiastical and historical links make the area into a unit.

2. The Nicene Creed, though a controversial summing up of Chalcedonian theology, seems to me a reasonable expansion of the creed agreed upon at Nicea in 325 C.E. The Armenian theologian Karekin Sarkissian discusses the views of the Oriental Orthodox Churches in his book *The Council of Chalceon and the Armenian Church* (1975). See also Gregorios et al. 1981; Pobee 1978, 81–98.

2. THE MODERN MISSIONARY MOVEMENT

1. The Evangelicals rightly put the well-being of Africans in the Africans own hands, and the resources to be tapped were also to be African. If the world is inter-dependent then let Africa supply her quota of what the world needs—good, but we are all aware of how this too has been bastardised. Later, on the Church scene the three Self-philosophies were to be developed and misused. In some countries, e.g., New Zealand, bishops protested against white governments and settlers who were grabbing land from the Maoris—this was the case in South Africa until the Church was silenced. The Churches taught farming and introduced other skills, but being Northern all this was geared to providing for the needs of the North—laying the grounds for the North-South debate on a just ordering of their economic relations and turning the attention of liberation theologians to the analysis of socio-economic and political context of Christian theology.

3. EXPRESSIONS, SOURCES, AND VARIANTS OF AFRICAN THEOLOGY

1. Compassion, according to the Akan, is situated in *yam* (bowels, stomach, the whole interior below the diaphragm). *Ayamuyie* (good interior) is kindness. Compassion here is therefore close to the Hebrew *rachamim*, compassion, which also means bowels. In Akan, the antithesis of *ayamuyie* is *ayamuowen* (bitter interior), stinginess, meanness, or unkindness. When specific, compassion is associated with the womb (abadae—where the foetus slept). Both fathers and mothers have abadae.

2. The male imagery of God becomes exaggerated when one translates Akan into English. The pronouns *Ọno* and *ne* are generic. But designating God as *Agya*, Father, is not a borrowing, though more commonly heard is *Nana* which stands for grandparent and is used to address rulers, divinities and other elders of the community.

3. Appleyard, the translator, says that by "the blind" is probably intended "humankind" or perhaps "the heathens." "Trumpet," he says, probably refers to church bells. I have borrowed the phrase "Sense and Nonsense about God" from the title of John Hall's contribution to SCM Senior Studies Series No. 1 (SCM Press, 1974). The problem of contextualisation includes that of translation, not only in terms of words but in ideas. In Akan ontology as in almost all of Black Africa 'Heaven' and 'Hell' of Christianity have no equivalents. See Mbiti in Dickson and Ellingworth for a discussion of eschatology and teleology.

4. Syncretism, with all the weight of a negative development, has become the whipping boy for those in departments of religious studies who advo-

cate dialogue with people of other faiths, African churches seeking to relate more dynamically to the cultures in which they live, and theologians in search of meaningful expressions of the faith.

5. In this respect compare the role played by the annual retelling of the exodus story in the Hebrew tradition (Deuteronomy 12). A similar reenactment of people's histories happens in many annual African festivals.

4. CONVENTIONAL DOGMATICS ON AFRICAN SOIL

1. "Primal" here stands for "first" (*primus*), and "primal religion" therefore refers to such religious beliefs and practices as were called forth by what was naturally experienced by people before other worldviews began to impinge upon theirs. I am indebted to J. V. Taylor (1973), author of *The Primal Vision: Christian Presence amid African Religion.*

2. See Baëta 1981. Increasingly this type of criticism of religious studies departments of African universities is being voiced. See also Kato 1975. At the 1982 conference of the West African Association of Theological Institutions, Dr. Onaiyekan, then rector of Saints Peter and Paul, Ibadan, stimulated discussion along lines similar to Baëta's and Kato's ideas. The title of his paper was "Higher Studies in Christian Religion in Nigeria: Points and Posers."

3. See Majeke 1962, 14. See also Majeke's foreword to Kato 1975 in which he concedes the presence of idolatry in the world beyond Africa.

5. THEOLOGY FROM A CULTURAL OUTLOOK

1. As Abram, he heeded a call to leave his native home, Ur of the Chaldeans. He did so not really knowing where he was going (Gn 12:1–4). For Christians and Muslims, as well as for Jews, Abraham has become the epitome of faith in action.

2. See Croatto 1981 for a contemporary exposition of the exodus in the Latin American context.

3. Western Christian understanding of history continues to be dominated by theories of church and state derived from historical situations in which the coin (Mt 22:17–21) and the two swords (Lk 22:38; Rom 13:4) are the models depicting the separate spheres of influence.

4. *Aladura,* "the Church of the Lord," is a church of Nigerian origin. It was founded by a Nigerian, but has branches all along the West Coast, in London, and in the United States. The main characteristic of this church is prayer; hence the designation *aladura,* "the praying ones." (*Adura* means "prayer" in Yoruba.) I use this name to include all the churches founded out of the charisma of African Christians because most of them exhibit an intense attachment to prayer. Recently I have also used the term

"the charismatic African churches" in order to highlight their emphasis on the charismatic gifts listed by Saint Paul, especially the speaking and interpretation of tongues and as originating from the charisma of Africans. The official designation of these churches is "African Independence Churches." The term raises a number of questions for me and I do not therefore wish to subscribe to it.

5. My personal reaction to a debate that took place in Lima during a discussion on the Eucharist.

6. Personal experiences gathered from my participation in the Community of Women and Men study undertaken by the World Council of Churches from 1978 to 1981.

6. CREATED AND REDEEMED

1. This is not entirely alien to the primal worldview of certain parts of Africa. The Igbo of Nigeria, for instance, lay great store on personal achievement. See Achebe 1959.

2. Although traditional rulers are never deposed for any reason whatsoever in some parts of Africa, in other parts this is always a possibility, as the rulers are constitutional monarchs. One cannot of course limit the impetus for the incessant coups d'etat in Africa to this view of government alone.

3. Whatever the arguments as to the settling of South Africa, it is clear that whites *came* from another continent and that blacks *belong* to the African continent. The philosophy that "occupation is nine-tenths of the law" cannot be allowed to go unchallenged.

4. God's rule through human agencies—including political parties, parliaments, and presidents—operates only as they recognize God as the true ruler and themselves as stewards. Hence the cautions of Revelations 13:18 and the call for wisdom.

5. Attestation of Hebrew antiquities aided by archeology has enhanced our understanding of the exodus and the settlement of Palestine. See comments by Alexander Jones, general editor of the *Jerusalem Bible*, pp. 10–11.

6. *Gye Nyame* is troublesome to translate as none of the English equivalents bring out the nuance of "without God all falls apart, returns to nothingness, becomes meaningless, yields no fruits, does not succeed." In Ghana "Except God" has become the accepted English formula.

7. EXCEPT GOD

1. *Borebore* is a praise-name that signifies God's creative activity. Modupe Oduyoye, in *The Sons of the Gods and the Daughters of Men* (1984) relates this Fante word to the Hebrew *'bo"re,'* "creator."

2. André Parrot, in *Noah's Ark* (1955, 9), gives what is no doubt an etiological story. It is of interest because the python features in not a few stories of "beginnings" in Africa.

3. In Gottwald 1979: See the major conclusions in the preface (p. xxiii), "Moses" (pp. 35–40), "Religious Idealism" (pp. 592–607), and "The 'Uniqueness' of Israel" (pp. 672–675).

4. *Racham* as used here could have been translated as "love"—hence my recalling Psalm 103 and John 3:16. On a continent being shaped by Christianity and Islam, *racham* becomes even more crucial in our theologia, for "compassion," one of the ninety-nine "beautiful names" of God, is of the same Semitic root.

5. *Adam*, from *adamah*, "earth-soil," leads to this rendition of the first human being (first *adam*) as a sexually undifferentiated being. See Gottwald (1979, 796–797, n. 628) for comments on Genesis 1:26–27.

6. Saint Paul's keen analysis of the human situation in this regard is apposite here. See also Romans 7, especially verses 22 and 23, noting that Paul is talking of what he has seen in his own life.

8. JESUS SAVES

1. If the Christian history of salvation includes a "fall" that is the result of distrust and self-seeking, then the Christ-event becomes the only antidote. This raises of course the question of whether the myth quality of the fall degrades the story of salvation in the Christ-event.

2. Literally *yeshuah* is made up of the root word meaning "to save," "to give safety, ease" (*yasha*) and of the personal name for God, Yahweh. The English version of the name is Joshua and means "Yahweh saves." Since salvation is seen as coming only from God, the word *yeshuah* has come to mean simply salvation, with no need to add "of God."

3. The word for deliver is *natsal*, "to snatch or take away"—another common word associated with God-in-Action.

4. In the context of the Akan worldview, atonement means reconciliation and is not concluded until the parties involved have joined in some act together such as sharing a meal. Such joint action is a pledge that the event that caused the discord will not be repeated. From this standpoint, picking any one theory of atonement does not satisfy the requirements for the rebuilding of community.

5. Gregory Baum discusses Karl Marx's insight into religion as being "the sigh of the oppressed creature, the heart of a heartless world, and the soul of a soul-less condition" (1975, 37). Note that only after the foregoing did Marx pronounce the now popular dictum that "religion is the opium of the people." The Africanist version of this dictum is: "They gave us the

Bible and took our land," and accuses Christianity of being an alienating religion.

9. COVENANT AND COMMUNITY

1. Among the Akan, the name a person is given depends on the day on which that person is born. The name given is known as the *kradin*, "soul-name." On the eighth day after birth at least one other name is added. One carries these names throughout life; marriage does not change them. These are the names ingrained on the personality and the only ones deemed spiritually efficacious.

10. FEMINISM

1. "Separate development" is the language apartheid South Africa resorted to in its attempt to justify the segregation of blacks into areas of the so-called homelands. I use the phrase here to show how the church often constituted itself in such a way that women and young people are put in separate groups as if only men formed the body of the church. Isolating women as a category reinforces what the wider community does to women. This discrimination has adverse effects on the full humanity and participation of women in the church and in society. Separate development then is for me a negative concept.

2. The Hebrew *Adam* is both generic, meaning human being, and specific, the personal name of the male partner of Eve. When to use male (man) and when to use human beings (people, persons) is a translation problem in both Old and New Testaments and has been an area of study by some feminist theologians. See, for instance, Russell 1976.

11. TRINITY AND COMMUNITY

1. Wiles 1967, 128. One cannot but agree with Wiles that this is modalism and that the only way to avoid this pitfall is to say: It has been imparted to us as a verbal disclosure about the inner nature of the godhead in scripture or the apostolic tradition.

2. I have taken a position that is hotly debated when applied to human community, especially to the organization of the church. See Williams 1966.

Bibliography

Abimbola, Wande. 1975. *Sixteen Great Poems of Ifa.* UNESCO.

Achebe, Chinua. 1959. *Things Fall Apart.* Greenwich, Conn.: Fawcett.

Adeyemo, Tokunbo. 1979. *Salvation in African Tradition.* Nairobi: Evangel Publishing House.

Anderson, W. B. 1963. *Ambassadors by the Nile.* London: Lutterworth Press.

Appiah-Kubi, Kofi, and Sergio Torres, eds. 1979. *African Theology en Route.* Maryknoll, N.Y.: Orbis Books.

Atiya, Aziz Suryal. 1948. *History of the Patriarchs of the Egyptian Church.* Cairo, Publications de la Société d'archéologie, copy—Textes et documents.

———. 1968. *History of Eastern Christianity.* London: Methuen. Indiana: University of Notre Dame Press. Also updated by author, Millwood, N.Y.: Kraus Reprint Co., 1980.

———. 1979. *The Copts and Christian Civilization.* Salt Lake City: Univeristy of Utah Press.

Baëta, C. G. 1960. "Lectures on Amos." Unpublished notes.

———. 1968. *Christianity in Tropical Africa.* London: Oxford University Press, International African Institute.

———. 1981. "Liberation Theology." Unpublished notes from tapes of the Danquah Memorial Lectures, Accra.

Baillie, John, et al., eds. 1953a. *Library of Christian Classics.* Vol. 3. London: SCM.

———. 1953b. *Library of Christian Classics.* Vol. 5. *Early Latin Theology* LCC/V. London: SCM.

Barkway, Lumsden. 1957. *The Creed and Its Credentials.* London: SPCK.

Bartels, F. L. 1965. *The Roots of Ghana Methodism.* Cambridge: Cambridge University Press, and Ghana: Methodist Book Depot.

Baum, Gregory. 1975. *Religion and Alienation.* New York: Paulist Press.

Becken, J. H., ed. 1973. *Relevant Theology for Africa.* Durban: Lutheran Publishing House.

Behr-Sigel, Elizabeth. n.d. "Woman Too Is in the Likeness of God." Unpublished CWMC Paper. Geneva: WCC.

p'Bitek, Okot. 1970. *African Religions in Western Scholarship*. Nairobi: East African Literature Bureau.

Boesak, Allan. 1972. *Farewell to Innocence: A Social-Ethical Study on Black Theology and Black Power*. Johannesburg. U.S. edition: Maryknoll, N.Y.: Orbis, 1976.

Bovill, E. W. 1933. *Caravans of the Old Sahara*. London: Oxford University Press. Quoted in Westermann 1935.

Brown, David. 1969. *The Divine Trinity: Christianity and Islam*. London: Sheldon Press.

Busia, K. A. 1951. *The Position of the Chief in the Modern Political System of Ashanti*. London: Oxford University Press.

Butcher, E. L. 1897. *History of the Church of Egypt*. London: Smith Elder.

Chioma, Filomena. 1978. "The Role of Women in Churches in Freetown, Sierra Leone." In *Christianity in Independent Africa*. Ed. Edward Fashole-Luke, et al. London: Collins.

Church Missionary Society (CMS). 1899. *One Hundred Years: Being the Short History of the Church Missionary Society*. 3d ed. London: CMS. Preface by Eugene Stock.

Croatto, J. Severino. 1981. *Exodus: Hermeneutics of Freedom*. Maryknoll, N.Y.: Orbis Books.

Cupitt, Don. 1977. "The Christ of Christendom." In Hick 1977, 133–147.

Desai, Ram, ed. 1962. *Christianity in Africa as Seen by Africans*. Denver: Allan Swallow.

Dickson, Kwesi A., and Paul Ellingworth. 1968. *Biblical Revelation and African Beliefs*. London: Lutterworth Press.

Evett, B. T. A. trans. 1895. *The Churches and Monasteries of Egypt and Some Neighboring Countries*, attributed to Abu Salîh the Armenian. Notes added by Alfred J. Butler. Oxford University Press. Clarendon Repro. 1969

Fabella, Virginia, ed. 1980. *Asia's Struggle for Full Humanity*. Maryknoll, N.Y.: Orbis Books.

Fabella, Virginia, and Sergio Torres, eds. 1977. *The Emergent Gospel: Theology from the Underside of History*. Maryknoll, N.Y.: Orbis Books.

———. 1983. *Irruption of the Third World: Challenge to Theology*. Maryknoll, N.Y.: Orbis Books.

Fey, Harold E., ed. 1976. *The Ecumenical Advance: A History of the Ecumenical Movement*. Vol. 2. London: SPCK.

Flannery, Austin, O.P., ed. 1966. *Vatican II: The Church Constitution: Texts and Commentaries.* Dublin: Scepter.

Frend, W. H. C. 1952. *The Donatist Church: A Movement of Protest in Roman Africa.* Oxford: Clarendon Press.

———. 1975. *Martyrdom and Persecution in the Early Church.* London: Blackwell's.

Gilli, Aldo. 1977. *Daniel Comboni: The Man and His Message.* Bologna: Editrice Missionaria Italia.

Gottwald, Norman K. 1979. *The Tribes of Yahweh: A Sociology of the Religion of Liberated Israel 1250–1050 B.C.E.* 1979. Maryknoll, N.Y.: Orbis Books.

Grau, E. 1968. "Missionary Policies as Seen in the Work of Missions with the Evangelical Presbyterian Church, Ghana." In Baëta 1968.

Gregorius, Paulos; W. H. Lazareth; and Nikos A. Nissiotis, eds. 1981. *Does Chalcedon Divide or Unite? Towards a Convergence in Orthodox Theology.* Geneva: WCC.

Gutiérrez, Gustavo. 1973. *A Theology of Liberation.* Maryknoll, N.Y.: Orbis Books.

Harnack, Adolf. n.d. *History of Dogma.* Vol. 2. trans. Neil Buchanan, Lond. William & Norgate, 1896.

Heasman, Kathleen. 1962. *Evangelicals in Action: An Appraisal of Their Social Work.* London: Geoffrey Bles.

Herzel, Susannah. 1981. *A Voice for Women.* Geneva: WCC.

Hewitt, Gordon. n.d. *The Problems of Success: A History of the CMS 1910–1942.* Vol. 1. London, S.C.M. Press 1971.

Hick, John, ed. 1977. *The Myth of God Incarnate.* London: SCM.

———. 1980. *God Has Many Names.* London: Macmillan.

Hodgson, Leonard. 1954. "The Doctrine of the Trinity: Some Further Thoughts." *Journal of Theological Studies,* New Series 5, part 1.

Horton, Robin. 1971. "African Conversions." *Africa* 41:85–108.

Hunter, William. 1962. *Christian Aṣọr Ndwon.* No. 103. Cape Coast: Methodist Book Depot.

Idowu, E. B. 1965a. *Olodumare: God in Yoruba Religion.* London: Longman; New York: Praeger, 1963.

———. 1965b. *Towards an Indigenous Church.* London: Oxford University Press.

———. 1973. *African Traditional Religion: A Definition.* London: SCM; Maryknoll, N.Y.: Orbis Books, 1973.

Ilevbare, J. A. 1980. *Carthage, Rome and the Berbers.* Ibadan: Ibadan University Press.

Jerome. *Epistles* CLVI 1:1, 5–7. In Stevenson 1975.

The Jerusalem Bible (JB). New York: Doubleday, 1966.

Jones, C. F. 1935. *A History of Ethiopia*. London: Oxford.

Kalu, Ogbu. 1977. "Church Presence in Africa." In Appiah-Kubi and Torres 1979.

Kato, Byang. 1975. *Theological Pitfalls in Africa*. Kisumu: Evangel Press.

Kupalo, Ancilla. 1978. *African Sisters Congregations: Realities of the Present Situation*, ed. Fashole–Luke, *Christianity in Independent Africa,* London: Collins, pp. 122–135.

Latourette, K. S. 1944. *A History of the Expansion of Christianity*. Vol. 6. *The Great Century: Northern Africa and Asia*. New York and London: Harper.

———. 1955. *A History of Christianity*. London: Eyre and Spottiswoode.

el Mahdi, Mandour. 1965. *A Short History of the Sudan*. London: Oxford University Press.

Majeke, Nosipho. 1962. "Role of the Missionaries in Conquests." In Desai 1962.

Mbiti, J. S. 1975. *Prayers of African Religion*. London: SPCK.

———. 1979. "The Biblical Basis for Present Trends in African Theology." In Appiah-Kubi and Torres 1979, 83–94.

Middle East Council of Churches. 1980. *Report of Consultation C. W.M.C.* Beirut.

Mikre-Selassie, G. A. 1976. *Church and Mission in Ethiopia: Relation to the Italian War and Occupation*. Ph.D. diss., Aberdeen.

Moore, Basil, ed. 1973. *Black Theology: The South African Voice*. London: C. Hurst.

Motte, Mary, and Joseph R. Lang. 1982. *Mission in Dialogue*. Maryknoll, N.Y.: Orbis Books.

Mugo, Erasto. 1975. *African Response to Western Christian Religion*. East Africa Literature Bureau.

Mveng, Engelbert. 1979. "Black African Art as Cosmic Liturgy and Religious Language." In Appiah-Kubi and Torres 1979, 137–142.

National Greater News. 1981. Newark, N.J. Black Christian Medium, Dec. 17, 1981.

Newbigin, Lesslie. 1978. *The Open Secret*. London: SPCK.

Ntwasa, Sabelo. 1973. "The Concept of God in Black Theology." In Moore 1973, 18–28.

Nyamiti, Charles. 1969. *African Theology: Its Nature, Problems and Methods*. Kampala: Gaba Publications.

Oduyoye, Amba. 1979. *Socialization through Proverbs: African Notes*. Ibadan: Institute of African Studies, University of Ibadan.

Oduyoye, Modupe. 1984. *The Sons of the Gods and the Daughters of Men*. Maryknoll, N.Y.: Orbis Books.

Ojike, Mbonu. 1955. *My Africa*. London: Blandford Press.

O'Neill, Colman, O.P. 1966. "The Mystery of the Church." In Flannery 1966.

Oosthuizen, C. G. 1979. *Iconography of Religions.* Leiden: E. J. Brill.

Oppong, Christine. 1976. *Consequences and Concomitants of Change: Issues Regarding the Relation to Family Structure.* Paper delivered at the Conference Centre, "Nigerian Women and Development in Relation to Changing Family Structure," University of Ibadan.

Parrinder, Geoffrey. 1961. *West African Religion.* London: Epworth Press.

Parrott, André. 1955. *Noah's Ark.* London: SCM.

Parvey, C. F. 1983. *The Community of Women and Men in the Church.* Geneva: World Council of Churches.

Plumb, J. H. 1955. *England in the Eighteenth Century (1714–1815).* New York: Penguin Books reprint.

Pobee, John S. 1976a. "Church and State in Ghana." In Pobee 1976b.

———. 1979. *Towards an African Theology.* Nashville, Tenn.: Abingdon.

———, ed. 1976b. *Religion in a Pluralistic Society.* Leiden: E. J. Brill.

Robinson, J. A. T. 1963. *Honest to God.* Philadelphia: Westminster Press.

Rotimi, Ola. 1979. *Kurunmi: A Historical Tragedy.* Ibadan: Oxford University Press.

Russell, Letty M. 1976. *The Liberating Word: A Guide to Nonsexist Interpretation of the Bible.* Philadelphia: Westminster Press.

Sankey, Ira David. 1907. *My Life and the Story of Gospel Hymns: Sacred Songs and Solos.* Philadelphia: Saturday School Times Co.; New York: AMS Press, 1974.

Sarkissian, Karekin. 1975. *The Council of Chalcedon and the Armenian Church.* New York: The Armenian Church Prelacy.

Sarpong, Peter. 1974. *Ghana in Retrospect.* Ghana Publishing.

Segundo, Juan Luis. 1976. *The Liberation of Theology.* Maryknoll, N.Y.: Orbis Books.

Shapiro, Max S., and Rhoda A. Hendricks. 1981. *A Dictionary of Mythologies.* London: Granada.

Soelle, Dorothee. 1974. *Political Theology.* Philadelphia: Fortress Press.

Sofola, Zulu. 1979. "The Theatre in Search for African Authenticity." In Appiah-Kubi and Torres 1979, 83–94.

Stevenson, J. 1974. *A New Eusebius: Documents Illustrative of the History of the Church to A.D. 337.* London: SPCK.

Taylor, J. V. 1963. *The Primal Vision: Christian Presence amid African Religion.* London: SCM; Philadelphia: Fortress Press, 1964.

Tertullian. *De Pudicitia.* In Baillie 1953b.

———. *On Women's Dress.* In *A Treasury of Early Christianity.* Ed. Anne Freemantle. New York: Viking, 1953.

Turner, Harold W. 1965. *Profile through Preaching: A Study of Sermon*

Texts Used in West African Independent Churches. London: Edinburgh House Press.

Turner, V. W. 1968. *The Drums of Affliction.* Oxford: Clarendon.

Van Alstyne, Frances Jane. 1962. [1933]. No. 338. In *Methodist Hymn Book.* 34th ed. London: Methodist Conference 1962 [1933].

Vidler, Alex. 1963. *Objections to Christian Belief.* London: Constable.

Visser't Hooft, W. A., ed. 1949. *The Ten Formative Years 1938–1948: First Assembly of the World Council of Churches, Amsterdam 1948.* London: SCM.

Wesleyan Missionary Notices (WMN). 1851. Vol. 3, 3d series, no. 37. Letter from the Revd. John Ayliff dated Herald-Town, Fort Beaufort 4/9/1856.

Westermann, Diedrich. 1935. *Africa and Christianity.* Duff Lectures. London, New York, Toronto: Oxford University Press. Repr. New York: AMS, 1977.

Wiles, M. 1967. *The Making of Christian Doctrine.* Cambridge: Cambridge University Press.

———. 1976. *What is Theology?* London: Oxford University Press.

Williams, Cornelius, O.P. 1966. Chapter 3 in Flannery 1966.

World Council of Churches (WCC). 1948. *Amsterdam Assembly Official Handbook.*

———. 1960. *One Lord, One Baptism.* Faith and Order Paper No. 29. London: SCM.

———. 1978. *Sharing in One Hope.* Faith and Order Paper No. 92. London: SCM.

Zoe-Obianga, Rose. 1983. "Resources in the Tradition for Renewal of Community." In Parvey 1983.

Index

Compiled by James Sullivan